Golden Fire

THE ANNIVERSARY BOOK OF THE OREGON SHAKESPEAREAN FESTIVAL

BY EDWARD & MARY BRUBAKER

WITH A PREFACE BY JERRY TURNER

Ashland

The Oregon Shakespearean Festival Association

International Standard Book Number 0-9614515-0-5
Library of Congress Catalog Number 85-2905
Copyright © 1985 by Oregon Shakespearean Festival Association
P.O. Box 158, Ashland, Oregon 97520 • 503/482-2111
Designer • Robert Reynolds
Editor • Kerry Hoover
Typesetting • Paul O. Giesey/Adcrafters
Printer • Graphic Arts Center
Bindery • Lincoln & Allen
Printed in the United States of America

Pacific Northwest Bell is proud to assist in the publication of this book, which is designed to increase awareness of the Oregon Shakespearean Festival.

Frontispiece: *Henry the Fifth*, 1982, the siege at Harfleur, Pat Patton, director.
Overleaf: *Much Ado About Nothing*, 1983, the final dance, Dennis Bigelow, director.
Photo Credit: Hank Kranzler.

— this majestical roof fretted with golden fire . . .

—HAMLET. 2.2

PREFACE

When a human being becomes a half-century old, it seems an occasion among family and friends to celebrate his accomplishments and vitality in having reached such a milestone. At fifty, a person has a lot to look back on. One is, generally, what one is going to be. The learning years are over; the years of mastery are at hand. There are many historical exceptions to this rule: One thinks of Shaw, for example, or Strindberg, whose post-Inferno period was perhaps his most creative. But rarely does it happen that the sixth decade of a person's life marks a period of undiscovered latent genius.

Is our institution, the Oregon Shakespearean Festival, like that? Of course our theatre is not really fifty years old. That is to say, 1985 does not mark fifty years of continuous production. The theatre was dark during the years of World War II. Still, we were founded in 1935, and to shave off the war years as not really counting is rather like a person reaffirming eternal youth because one looks younger than one is. "Well preserved" is not a flattering description of an institution any more than it is of an individual.

I do not mean to imply that being fifty is something to be ashamed of. Not at all. For an institution to have survived half a century with vigor intact has to mean there was something extraordinarily vital in the enterprise. Few institutions (or ideas) last that long. Dr. Stockman of *An Enemy of the People* thought a really good idea might last twenty years before it was replaced by something new. Being half a century old is something to crow about. Still, there is something disquieting about "the second fifty years."

For one thing, an institution, like a person, carries the burden of its history, or the wisdom of its experience, whichever you prefer. It is easier to trace past developments than to detect the paths of the future. Decisions made in the cloudy present have a way of seeming much clearer in the light of history. The building of the Angus Bowmer Theatre, for example, which seems to us now such a triumphantly correct thing to do, was at the time a monumental risk. The Bowmer changed the fundamental nature of the Festival and to many, such change seemed foolhardy and wrongheaded. The wiser heads (Bill Patton's for one) saw the decision as easy to make, since they saw that to continue to be a summer Shakespeare festival with limited capacity outdoors was to flirt with bankruptcy. We had to change; we had to grow; or die.

Many of the most fundamental decisions of the past fifty years seem to me to have been made that way. They represent, as it were, a triumph of pragmatism and practice over theory. The whole idea, for example, of a Shakespeare theatre based upon a reconstruction of the Fortune Playhouse taking root in a small Southern Oregon town is theoretically preposterous. Could there possibly be enough antiquarians around these parts to support such an exotic enterprise? Could Ashland hope to do what London showed no interest in doing? Or Stratford-upon-Avon?

The truth is, of course, that antiquarian reconstruction was only part of the project. William Poel's idea, the Elizabethan Stage Society, did not advocate literal reconstruction of the "open" stage for its own sake. Nor did his disciple, B. Iden Payne, develop his "modified Elizabethan" plan merely for authenticity. Nor were Angus Bowmer's plans in Ashland designed to capture the imaginations of the historically inclined. All three were more interested in mining the rich resources of Shakespeare's imaginative world in ways made more vivid and with greater force and clarity than the conventional proscenium arch theatre would allow. There was more actor than archeologist in each of these three men, and the public responded to the liberation of Shakespeare's verse far more than to the archaic "quaintness" of architectural reconstruction.

There were, and are, a certain number of our audience who come to Ashland to seek "authentic" productions of the Bard. In an age when radical editing to fit a director's concept is commonplace; where even historians like A. L. Rowse advocate rewriting the master's texts to conform to the contemporary usage, it is natural to find people in search of "the real thing." Such people admire the relatively uncut productions of the outdoor stage, the rapid flow of scene against scene, and the pageantry and pomp of Elizabethan decor. But far larger in number are the people who discover in Ashland the power and glory of Shakespeare's art on stage. To them, it matters less that a production is authentically correct (a goal that can never be achieved) than that it is interesting, exciting, and clear in ways almost impossible to achieve in the classroom. It may still be a literary

experience handsomely and sumptuously illustrated through theatrical means, but the work somehow makes a transformation from chore to pleasure, from homework to sensual delight. The opening of doors to previously inaccessible treasures is no mean achievement for any theatre.

So far, I have spoken of Shakespeare and the Elizabethan stage as if that were the special and exclusive dramatic menu of Ashland. If that were true once, it is not true now. The building of the Angus Bowmer Theatre, and later the Black Swan, enlarged our repertory and expanded our mission. In 1985, I believe, we are dealing with something far more fundamental than making Shakespeare palatable or illustrating dramatic classics: We are, together with our audience, finding a theatrical language appropriate to our times.

The vitality of a play depends neither on its historical interest nor upon its capacity to capture the social issues of the moment. Its vitality is found in what it has to say and how it says it. A great play cries to be performed; it is less literature than action. It speaks, as it were, in subtext as well as text; in mime and gesture as well as words. A vital theatre is one that organizes those special characteristics of the performer to express in a language of action those crises of emotion that have meaning both to the audience and to the playwright. A vital classic is one that unites the permanency of its statement with the immediacy of audience perception. Theatre at its best defines the human condition in roles both traditional and relevant.

What seems much clearer to us now, when three very different spaces each have plays in rotating repertory, is that close attention to the central dramatic conflict in a play is more important than the space it plays in. Many in our audience prefer the intimacy of the Black Swan where subtleties and ambiguities are readily apparent. A classic play will always contain such subtleties and ambiguities. It's part of what makes them classic. *The Taming of the Shrew* on the surface is a lesson on how to break and harness the untamed energies of a high-spirited woman to the needs of her man and master. *The Merchant of Venice* is a fairytale romance of love and money which also demonstrates how an infidel Jew can be outwitted and defeated. To modern sensibilities the first is anti-feminist, the second anti-Semitic. One can, and some of our patrons do, justify both as illustrations of social attitudes now discarded. The conflicts have historical, but not contemporary significance.

I think such an approach does a disservice both to the plays and to the potential power of the theatre. Katherine and Shylock are truly more than their archetypes: Shrew and Jew, and a good production, a responsible production, will demonstrate that. A classical play, done in whatever space, will have something immediate to say to an audience as well as an historical frame of how it is said. A dramatic production should always be more than an historical reproduction.

The Black Swan came into existence partly out of a desire to expand our repertory beyond the conventional bounds of classical revivals. A playwright need not be dead to be worthy, nor does the purity of the past take on any tarnish of the present when juxtaposed with the work of today's theatrical practitioners. On the contrary, the measure of a work of art may best be seen in such a context. Our future may well see more attention to the work of living writers.

It is perhaps too simplistic to say that the Festival history up to 1985 was devoted to demonstrating the thesis that an author's work can best be understood in the context of the period and stage conditions for which he wrote. If that were true, Ibsen, Chekhov and Shaw would be lost in obscurity on the presentational platform so suited to Marlowe, Shakespeare and Brecht. What is closer to fact is that the pioneering work of Ashland's "open" stage swept away a goodly portion of accumulated stage tradition, allowing directors and performers to deal with the heart of the dramatic action in a more direct way.

The great writers speak from their era, but not always about it. Rather they are likely to be preoccupied with certain eternal truths of the heart in tragic or comic conflict. Thus, *King Lear* is neither about prehistoric Britain, nor Elizabethan society, but about loyalty and betrayal in the face of growing old. We and the author share a common humanity in that theme, and can share a common understanding through a theatrical image of it. But no single stage or manner of production is ideally suited to express it all. The task we must set for ourselves is to present the conflict that lies within and behind the trappings of the drama and of the stage. We must try to make clear and forceful to the contemporary audience the intent of the author's vision, which may be of another time, another place, and certainly in another manner.

We can depend upon one thing: Fifty years from now our efforts will seem crude, overly simple, and quaint. Sometimes they will seem to have been misguided, or downright boneheaded. Still, there is consolation in the permanence and transmutability of the classics. Moliere will still be produced; so will Aeschylus and Shaw and O'Neill; so will Shakespeare and Sheridan and Ibsen. I have a hunch the Oregon Shakespearean Festival will still be hanging in there with artists and audiences still seeking to find the right and appropriate mode. We oldtimers may well not like those productions, nor understand them very well. Some of our favorites will have dropped out of the repertory, discarded or neglected as having no function in the new age. There will be new voices to which we never could relate, and revivals of plays we never thought would last.

1985 is the fiftieth year of prologue to discovery. Let's drink to the past.

1986 will be the first year of preface to the future. How about a toast for tomorrow?

—JERRY TURNER, *Artistic Director*

13

Hank Kranzler

Hank Kranzler

Opposite: *A Midsummer Night's Dream*, 1979,
Dennis Bigelow, director. Stuart Duckworth,
Oberon; Joan Stuart-Morris, Titania.
Above: *Two Gentlemen of Verona*, 1981,
David Ostwald, director.
Right: Paul Vincent O'Connor as a pedant
in *The Taming of the Shrew*, 1984,
Pat Patton, director.

Left: The curtain call for *Tartuffe*, 1978, Sabin Epstein, director.

Top: *What the Butler Saw*, 1983. Mrs. Prentice (Priscilla Hake Lauris) pulls a gun on Dr. Prentice (Philip Davidson) while Nicholas Beckett (Daniel Mayes) dives for cover.

Center: *The Time of Your Life*. 1974. Joe (James Edmondson), Arab (Ernie Stewart), Kit Carson (Mark Murphey) and Nick (Michael Kevin).

Bottom: *Troilus and Cressida*, 1984. Richard E. T. White, director; William Bloodgood, settings; Michael Olich, costumes.

Hank Kranzler

Hank Kranzler

The Wild Duck, 1979. The Ekdal family, Hedvig
(Cameron Dokey), Hjalmar (John Shepard),
and Gina (Fredi Olster).

Mother Courage and Her Children, 1978. Eilif
(Rick Hamilton) and Swiss Cheese (Richard
Farrell) pull the wagon and passengers,
Mother Courage (Margaret Rubin) and Kattrin
(Terry Hays).
Right: The curtain call for *Wild Oats*, 1981,
Jerry Turner, director; music composed and
directed by Todd Barton.

Left: Denis Arndt as Archie Rice in
The Entertainer, 1983.
Above: J. Wesley Huston as John and James
Avery as Winston in *The Island,* 1981.
Center: Mary Turner as Laura in *The Father,*
1982.
Below: Charlie (Harry Woolf) and Nancy (Mary
Turner) meet the lizards, Sarah (Maureen
Kilmurry) and Leslie (Rex Rabold) in *Seascape,*
1980.

Hank Kranzler

Gentles, perchance you wonder at this show;
But wonder on till truth make all things plain.
—A MIDSUMMER NIGHT'S DREAM. 5.1.

William Shakespeare wrote his plays over a quarter of a century; his company produced them over forty-five years. The Oregon Shakespearean Festival observes its Golden Anniversary in 1985 by honoring its past and celebrating its future.

Altogether it is an unusual institution, not least for the way it has developed. The beginnings were necessarily difficult and limited, though from the first there was the exciting prospect that larger and better things could be accomplished and a determination to pursue them. That prospect and determination carried the Festival forward to its present position of prominence and continue to characterize its work today.

Those who remember the work and the joy of mounting the first Festival season, *The Merchant of Venice* and *Twelfth Night* in 1935, find Ashland in the 1980s an incredible scene. George Francis Smith, who played Malvolio that first time, expressed his reaction this way:

> It seems so fabulous that I find it difficult to believe. I see it's there; I know it's true, but the fact that it all happened is a little difficult for me to comprehend even yet.
> —INTERVIEW WITH NORA YEOMAN. 10/15/80

Angus Bowmer, the Festival's founder and its artistic director for thirty-five years, was perhaps the least surprised by what the Festival eventually became. He saw the possibilities more fully than anyone, and he knew first-hand how it all happened from a lifetime of adroit pushing and planning to build a major theatre. But in recalling the way things looked at the start, even he sounded a note of wonder at the transformation. In his autobiographical history of the Festival he wrote:

> Only the innocence of youth could have engendered such improbable visions as we had. In my own inexperience I was the blind leading the blind. But out of such unlikely beginnings we now have a theatre whose influence is felt across the English speaking world.
> —AS I REMEMBER, ADAM. P.69.

Today first-time visitors to Ashland, although they may have heard much about the Festival from a friend, or by reading about

Hank Kranzler

Left: The Festival's founder, Angus L. Bowmer.
Above: On the Festival grounds, the outdoor Elizabethan stage on the left and the indoor Angus Bowmer Theatre on the right.

it, are certain to be surprised by what they see. Their immediate reaction is one of delight at the quality of the productions. As one from Washington state wrote on a card, "Outstanding, I never really understood Shakespeare before!" A visitor from California wrote, "The Ashland Festival is absolutely the best bet for theatre, atmosphere, and friendly people of anywhere in the country."

Looking at facts about Ashland in statistical form is no less surprising than a first impression of the productions. Here is a company devoted to classical drama, operating three theatres with a repertory of eleven new productions each season. From February to November there are some 600 performances with a total attendance of over 300,000. The company—counting the artistic and administrative staff, the directors and designers, the managers for stage, house, and office, the performers, technicians, craftsmen, and the crews for costume, staging, box office, and maintenance—numbers over 300 and they are backed by some 800 volunteer workers. In addition, the Festival Association has some 8,000 contributing members.

How is it possible that a place so small and so remote could be endowed with such theatrical riches? This is not simply a question about Ashland as a place on the map, it is also a question about the people and policies that contribute to the unlikely and unusual success of the Festival.

I like this place
And willingly could waste my time in it.
—AS YOU LIKE IT. 2.4.

Kathy Hollis Cooper

Southern Oregon is a region of remarkable natural beauty. Ashland, one of the most attractive towns in the area, lies to the west of the Cascade range on a northern slope of the Siskiyou ridge that separates Oregon and California.

Ashland Creek reaches deep into the Rogue River National Forest for melted snows that flow brawling over granite boulders and relaxing pools. On the narrow flats that border the creek there are a series of groves that make refreshing retreats in the dry summer months. And here, going back to the time when history and legend meet, the tribes of the area gathered for the sacred dances that marked their festive days.

In 1851 the discovery of gold at nearby Jacksonville brought a rush of pioneers and adventurers who forced the Indians out of the area. Before long the groves bordering Ashland Creek were being used again as a gathering place, only this time by picnickers and campers seeking a respite from the heat in towns and farms

The slopes of Mt. Ashland in Spring.
Right: The Chautauqua campgrounds,
Ashland, 1909.

Chautauqua Auditorium
Ashland Oregon.

spread across the broad valley of Bear Creek to the north of Ashland and east of Jacksonville.

The town of Ashland grew up around a sawmill built on the creek. Later there was a flour mill and a woolen mill. Unlike its boomtown neighbor, Ashland seems to have been more orderly and certainly less crowded than Jacksonville. Even then it was described as a good place to raise a family. In the first issue of *The Ashland Tidings*, the editor described the town of 1876 in these words:

> There is no church and no saloon, but whiskey is sold by the bottle and preaching is done in the schoolhouse; and therefore, the people are generally happy.

Certainly Ashland was a town that went in for self-improvement. In 1872 an institution of higher learning was opened by the Methodist minister. Although it had a fitful early history, sometimes called the Academy, sometimes the College, it was the foundation of the present-day Southern Oregon State College. By 1891 when members of the Epworth League started the town library, Ashland had its famous City Band, wooden sidewalks, six churches, a suitable number of saloons, hotels, and an Opera House. The beautiful park which now ornaments the creek was begun in 1902 when the Women's Civic Improvement Club and the Ladies' Chautauqua Club made a concerted effort to improve the campgrounds.

Mention of the Chautauqua Club takes us a little ahead of our story. As its name suggests it was organized to support the association sponsoring the annual Chautauqua assemblies in Ashland. Originating in Lake Chautauqua, New York, the programs were designed to provide educational and cultural activities to rural areas during the slack time between planting and harvest. It was almost inevitable that Ashland would develop a Chautauqua of its own. By 1890 it was the largest town in Southern Oregon, conveniently on the main rail line that linked Portland and San Francisco, and it already was a resort with hotels, rooming houses, and camping sites for summer visitors.

A Chautauqua assembly was very much like a Methodist camp meeting with the addition of concerts, lectures, dramatic readings, classes, and discussion groups. In Ashland the activities were usually scheduled for ten days in July. In addition to the series of attractions that drew crowds to the auditorium, the days were filled with classes in bible study, literature, singing, cooking, crafts, physical training and eurythmics.

Although programs tended to keep the wicked stage at arm's length, there were moments of flirtation in that direction. Besides

Left: The Chautauqua auditorium, 1918.
Overleaf: Annually the "Feast of the Tribe of Will," held in Lithia Park (formerly the Chautauqua grounds) marks the opening of the outdoor Elizabethan stage.
Photo Credit: Hank Kranzler

31

the standard cantatas, the chorus worked up concert perform-
ances of Verdi's *Il Trovatore* and Gilbert and Sullivan's *H.M.S.
Pinafore*. And the celebrities who came—singers like Madame
Schumann-Heink, entertainers like Sir Harry Lauder, orators like
William Jennings Bryan, and concert bands like John Philip
Sousa's—each brought their special qualities of showmanship and
glamour.

From the beginnings in 1893, the Ashland Chautauqua drew
crowds. An auditorium to accommodate a thousand was built on
the hill above the plaza and adjacent to the park. It had to be
enlarged by 1901 and again in 1918 when attendance at the major
events rose to three thousand.

As the introduction of the automobile, radio, and film altered
the tempo and routine of American life, the appeal of Chautauqua
programs slackened. Unfortunately, expenses continued to
increase so that even a slight diminution of attendance made it
impossible for scheduling to continue. Ashland's Chautauqua
reached that point in 1925. The wooden dome of the auditorium,
once advertised as the largest west of the Rockies, had become a
white elephant. A few years later, like the movement it sym-
bolized, the dome began to sag and had to be taken down to
prevent its collapse.

Only the circular, concrete foundation remained. It is still
there, under a tangle of ivy and sporting a crown of banners, a
huge wall embracing the auditorium of the Festival's outdoor
Elizabethan stage.

I serve here voluntary.

—TROILUS AND CRESSIDA. 2.1.

Although ten years were to pass before the Festival made its
first entrance in 1935, the legacy of the Chautauqua was certainly
more than an enclosure where audiences and actors might come
together and share the wonders of Shakespeare under the stars.

For one thing the officers and trustees of the Chautauqua
Association were drawn from nearby towns—Jacksonville, Medford, Central Point, Grants Pass, as well as Ashland—and they
spread a wide net to recruit individuals and organizations to help
in selling tickets and to take on the work of preparation and
promotion. It was very much a community effort with Ashland as
host, only in this case the community skipped over municipal
boundaries. Because of Chautauqua many people in Southern
Oregon and Northern California came to think of Ashland as their
community too. They went there to celebrate the Fourth of July,
and for picnics, barbecues, and band concerts in the summer. Big

Matthew Harrison Brady (Wayne Ballantyne)
welcomed to Hillsboro in *Inherit the Wind*, 1982,
directed by Dennis Bigelow. The character of
Brady is modeled on William Jennings Bryan,
the famous orator.
Right: Mr. and Mrs. William Jennings Bryan
surrounded by the welcoming committee,
Chautauqua campgrounds, Ashland, 1907.

doings in Ashland were always likely to draw participants and spectators from all over.

This is not to say that the Festival inherited an audience and a cadre of volunteers. Those things had to be rebuilt, but a tradition of broad community support and individual effort was there to build on.

Most volunteer work is now formally organized. Including the Festival Board of Directors and the Trustees of the Endowment Fund, there are currently fourteen groups whose members commit themselves to a regular schedule. They are most in evidence at the height of the summer season in the great outdoor Elizabethan Theatre. They serve as ticket takers, hostesses and ushers, work at the refreshment stands, peddle tarts and toffees, rent pillows, blankets and "Elizabethan rain capes" when showers threaten. Many wear costumes which add to the holiday spirit of the crowd gathered to watch the pre-show entertainment provided by the Festival musicians and dancers. The most colorful group is the Redcoats, who assist the house managers, and are organized under captains and elect a president and an officer called Sir Toby Belch.

The Festival's principal auxiliary is the Tudor Guild, begun in 1948. It has over one hundred members whose fund raising activities make it a major financial contributor to the Festival. Other groups volunteer at the information booth and the Exhibit Center and help with mailings and office work. All told, volunteers number about eight hundred, carrying on a rich tradition of value beyond calculation.

Similarly, by long established custom the agencies of local government, the schools and college, the chamber of commerce and businesses, the service and social clubs support the Festival in many ways as a matter of course. Such contributions do more than stretch the production budget; they create the very spirit of community celebration that lies at the heart of a theatre.

This tradition was evident from the very beginning of the Festival. Maxine Hunnell came from Grants Pass for the first four seasons to work on costumes or "anything else that had to be done." She tells of using fabric that people would donate, of going through many trunks "on Granite Street and other streets in the town looking for materials and buttons and braid and all that sort of thing." They were able to get First World War long underwear to use for tights from Perrine's Department Store at ten cents a pair. They dyed, painted, and stenciled muslin, Canton flannel, and burlap to make brocades, velvets, and theatre curtains. They made do with a costume budget of twenty dollars. That and a lot of volunteer work worth many times the value of the donated or discounted materials. To bed after midnight and to work by seven. Maxine remembers her mother saying, "You are crazy to

Left: The Festival dancers who entertain nightly before performances on the Elizabethan stage.

work that hard for nothing." Nothing? It was true, Maxine admits:

> We didn't get paid a cent for anything we did during those years. And as I have said so often since then, that I did not work for nothing because that experience and those associations have compounded over and over again, even today.

—INTERVIEW WITH JOE KOGEL. 5/3/83

Today Maxine Hunnell is still volunteering at the Tudor Guild Shop, at the Exhibit Center, and as a hostess in the outdoor theatre.

When the Festival company was entirely volunteer, most of them were from the area, students or teachers who gave up ordinary summer vacations or paying jobs for one of love's labours. After the Second World War, following the lead of the Tudor Guild, contributions by individuals, service clubs, and foundations made some "scholarships" available to actors and technicians which made it possible for the company to be recruited from greater distances. These stipends were helpful in meeting expenses, but everyone had to adopt a tight budget to get through the summer with something left over for the bus fare home. When in some cases the money ran out, the only resource would be the funds for no-interest loans managed by the Tudor Guild.

A spare life makes a mark and so did the members of the company on the Ashland streets. You could spot them a block away, not simply for carrying a script and reciting Shakespeare aloud, but partly from their manifest independence and partly from dressing to suit themselves rather than the fashion. After all, in the fifties a man in long hair and a woman in leotards made a spectacle. They came to be called Shakespeares, sometimes in derision and sometimes as a salute to their dedication.

Once in a while the kids in town might make a bid for attention by running past the theatre yelling, "Hey Shakespeare! Romeo, Oh Romeo!" More often, because rehearsals were open, the kids with nothing to do came through the gate and found themselves drawn into the Shakespearean circle. They always sat in the front row.

When the lumberjacks came to town on Saturday nights getting in digs at the Shakespeares was one way they had of making contact. For their part the Shakespeares liked adventure too, so after rehearsal when they showed up at Cook's Reception, the tavern just downhill from the theatre, things could get tense. But evenings at Cook's usually followed a different scenario. An actor like Michael O'Sullivan who could tap a long repertory of stories and jokes would begin an impromptu entertainment and before long the Shakespeares would be treated to a round of beer.

Festival archive

Jim Chrisman

Above: Children take front row seats for an open rehearsal on the Elizabethan stage, 1953.
Below: The souvenir shop run by the Tudor Guild on the Festival grounds.
Right: Crowds gather before performances in the outdoor theatre to hear the Festival musicians.

The community did much more than serve up an occasional round to say thank you to the Shakespeares. Although not part of any official schedule, a tradition of parties and picnics developed that the company could count on for fun and food. The night the company first assembled, Bev and Jean Cope had a get-together at their home. Next, after the cast lists were pinned on the call board the Tudor Guild gave a "casting blues" supper in the Episcopal Parish House. Every kitchen in Ashland seems to have sent over a dish. After supper Gertrude Bowmer would stand up and introduce the whole company one by one with a word on where they came from—a feat no one else could have done that early in the summer. On days off during the rehearsal period, Mrs. Bowmer prepared picnics to Crater Lake, Union Creek, the California redwoods, and the Oregon beaches. Later in the summer there were after-theatre suppers hosted by Leila Parker at her cafe in Talent, by Julie Tummers at her restaurant in Central Point, and by Kim's in Medford. Mr. and Mrs. Alfred Carpenter regularly gave a luncheon and swim party at their home in Jacksonville. And when peaches were ripe, Mr. and Mrs. Frank Davis gave their annual pancake brunch in the backyard of their home in Ashland.

At these affairs—and there were many others from time to time—the company was made to feel at home. The best illustration of that is the story of the actor who arrived at an open house and asked his hostess if she had a shower. She did, and he took one before joining the party.

As the company grew such personal hospitality became a thing of the past. But the sense of personal attachment to the Festival by the community, almost of personal ownership, continues. Expressed in hours of volunteer work, it rubs off on the thousands who have come to make Ashland their town for theatre.

Here's a marvelous convenient place for our rehearsal. This green plot shall be our stage, this hawthorne-brake our tiring house; and we will do it in action as we will do it before the Duke.

—A MIDSUMMER NIGHT'S DREAM. 3.1

These words of Peter Quince must have taken on a personal significance for Angus Bowmer when he played the role in 1961. While speaking them he was standing in that marvelous convenient place where almost thirty years earlier the dream of a Festival took hold of his imagination.

Way back then it could hardly have seemed convenient to the

Left: Angus Bowmer as Peter Quince, surrounded by the mechanicals, in *A Midsummer Night's Dream*, 1961, directed by B. Iden Payne.

ordinary observer. The domed roof of the Chautauqua auditorium had been taken down; the remaining foundation walls enclosed an arena of packed earth that had gone back to being a field again. Weeds grew wild in summer and wilted in the wet winter. The place was a mess. But Angus Bowmer was no ordinary observer; the walls reminded him of the circular theatres pictured in maps of Elizabethan London.

Another circumstance connects the 1961 production of *A Midsummer Night's Dream* with the origins of the Festival and explains why Angus Bowmer saw an Elizabethan stage when he looked at the Chautauqua shell. That year *Dream* was directed by Ben Iden Payne, the man who introduced Angus to the possibilities of staging Shakespeare in the Elizabethan manner. That was in 1930, the year before he came to Ashland to teach at the normal school. He was studying at the University of Washington when Payne was there as a guest director. Angus played Boyet in *Love's Labour's Lost*, played bits and stage managed *Cymbeline* under Payne's direction. Working on those two productions was a full, practical, and inspiring course in Shakespearean theatre from a director of extraordinary experience.

Iden Payne was the founder of the Manchester Repertory Company, the pattern for regional repertories in England. In his earlier career as an actor he came to know the work of William Poel, an eccentric, innovative director, and invited him to stage *Measure for Measure* for the Manchester company. The production, with Poel as Angelo, Sara Allgood as Isabella, and Payne as Lucio, went well enough to be taken to Stratford-upon-Avon for the Festival of 1908.

Payne recognized the value of Poel's way of doing Shakespeare's plays and adopted it when he came to stage them himself in New York, at a variety of American universities, and at England's Stratford Festival which he directed from 1935 to 1942, the years Angus Bowmer produced his initial seasons at Ashland.

The best way to describe the Poel-Payne-Bowmer approach to Shakespearean production is to say that it was developed in reaction against what had become the traditional method that distorted the plays in a variety of ways. Essentially they were revamped to make them fit the modern picture-frame theatre, the proscenium arch. Producers looked for opportunities for elaborate scenic effects and the star actors wanted opportunities to show off their strong points. If the plays had to be cut, rewritten, and rearranged to bring off these great effects, the distortion went unnoticed or seemed worthwhile. It was accepted that Shakespeare needed modern improvements. Even his best friends thought he was a better poet than playwright. It must be said that the great actors did give their audiences moments of grandeur and excitement, and that their designers and technicians accom-

The Swan Theatre in Shakespeare's London, from a drawing by J. de Witt, c. 1596.
Right: B. Iden Payne played Friar Lawrence in *Romeo and Juliet* at the Festival in 1956. Rosalyn Newport was Juliet and Ted van Griethuysen, Romeo.

40

plished marvels of illusion and illustration. These triumphs of the Victorian actor-managers gave their traditional methods enormous influence and prestige.

William Poel looked at the whole matter differently. He organized the Elizabethan Stage Society in 1893 to test his theories in amateur productions of the dramas of Shakespeare and his contemporaries. Poel came to believe that the best way to do a Shakespearean play was in a manner approximating the conditions of its original production. In short, he wanted to use an Elizabethan stage for an Elizabethan play.

It was a logical and simple idea, even when we recognize that we don't know very exactly what an Elizabethan stage may have been like. But at the time Poel began his campaign for simpler methods, his ideas seemed very odd, largely because it meant marching backward to the bare platform, the empty stage without scenery depicted in the drawing of the Swan Theatre of Shakespeare's day. No one who believed in progress or that Shakespeare could be done at all, believed he deserved such bald and negligent treatment. Or to describe the difficulty differently, Poel was saying that if the plays were allowed to speak in their own way, following the form Shakespeare designed, they would be better than the versions revamped for the modern stage, better than the versions in which Booth and Irving had triumphed.

Poel had his defenders from the start—Bernard Shaw was one —and as directors became more interested in simplified, innovative staging, replacing realistic scenery with decor that was frankly theatrical, productions in the Elizabethan manner gradually succeeded in demonstrating that there was something to be said for the new approach.

The tradition that Angus Bowmer brought to Ashland was characterized by a desire to do the plays as written, to find a way to make them work. The Elizabethan stage constructed in the Chautauqua shell was a means to that end. Neither Payne nor Bowmer were antiquarians who had searched and researched for the dimensions of a lost original. They were practical men of the theatre and the stage configuration they used—an open platform with pillars supporting a shadowing roof, two side entrances, inner stages, and a balcony—was adopted because it allowed a flowing transition from one scene to the next without distractions. In the flow of action, Shakespeare's arrangement of scenes revealed new meaning and excitement.

Payne put this emphasis on the matter:

> My intention was simply to adhere to what Poel's production of *Measure for Measure* had taught me: that the fundamental quality of a Shakespearean production should be complete fluidity of action.
>
> —A LIFE IN A WOODEN O. P. 62

Cymbeline, 1956, B. Iden Payne, director. From left, Ted van Griethuysen, Guiderius; Joan Darling, Imogen; Eberle Thomas, Arviragus; Brad Curtis, Belarius.

Mr. Payne was a courteous, considerate person of the old school who raised his voice only for matters that seemed to him of the greatest urgency. "What are you waiting for?" he would shout when actors hesitated off-stage. "No, dear, you must come in on the beat!" The word "dear" was a sure sign that he was being nice under duress.

Angus Bowmer used to say that Shakespeare invented the film technique of the lap-dissolve, that his scenes were meant to overlap, one beginning and drawing the attention of the audience to another area of the stage almost before the last line of the preceding scene had been spoken. He was so confident that Shakespeare's plays were designed for continuous, uninterrupted movement like a movie, that he ran the Festival performances without intermissions. With audiences seated outdoors, the need to stretch the legs or go out for a smoke was not there, so the innovation was readily accepted.

Producing Shakespeare well involves a lot more than the deft management of exits and entrances so that the action can flow in a steady rhythm, but it has an impact far beyond what the audience or the critics would think possible. The same problems for an affecting performance have to be solved by actors and directors as in working with any script. Expressive speech and movement must be developed; the moments for emphasis and varied pacing must be found; the drama of character and conflict must be realized. As actors, Poel, Payne, and Bowmer were aware of these problems from an actor's point of view. What was new in their approach was the configuration of playing places in the Elizabethan stage that allowed what Bowmer called "the story telling rhythm" of Shakespearean drama to be realized in a way that conventional staging distorted.

Another advantage of their method was that it placed a fuller trust in the imagination of the audience. The actors played on a platform in front of an ornamental facade rather than within a stage setting. The platform could become as Peter Quince describes it, "a green plot with a hawthorne brake behind it," without being defined by the brush of a scene painter or by the ingenuity of a stage carpenter. This direct appeal to the imagination made the audience more fully participants in the making of the play, and gave the drama a freshness and immediacy that the proscenium arch could not evoke.

The blank wall of the Chautauqua shell was indeed a marvelous, convenient place to begin a Shakespearean Festival.

Ashland's first Elizabethan stage, 1935.

Soon after Angus Bowmer joined the faculty of Southern
Oregon State College, then Southern Oregon State Normal
School, word spread in Ashland that the new instructor was
directing plays worth seeing. Meanwhile, the new instructor was
taking the measure of the community. He guessed it might support a Shakespearean Festival.

Bowmer persuaded a group of business and professional men
with whom he met on Tuesday nights to work with the city to
expand the Fourth of July celebrations and he volunteered to
prepare a repertory of plays as part of the scheme. The streets
would be decorated and crowded with visitors, a potential
audience he could not hope to gather on his own.

As a W.P.A. project, the city built the Elizabethan stage he
needed inside the Chautauqua arena. On the back of an envelope
he sketched from memory the layout of the stage he had helped
build for Iden Payne's productions at the University of Washington. For the repertory his spring production at the college, *The
Merchant of Venice*, would be revived for one performance and two
performances of *Twelfth Night* would open and close the three-day
Festival, July 2 to 4, 1935.

The unexpected success of the Festival is well illustrated by an
oft repeated story. Here is the first part of the story as Angus
recalled it:

> About two weeks before the Fourth of July I was
> visited by a delegation from the celebration com-
> mittee. They opened the conversation by assuring
> me . . . that they had nothing against Shakespeare,
> and that furthermore they thought the presentation
> of his plays was rather a good thing for the commu-
> nity. But they went on to express their concern for a
> possible deficit in the celebration's budget. That
> this would be a deplorable situation we all agreed.
> The way they approached the subject made it clear
> that they expected me to object. Thus it came to
> them as a great relief when I agreed to allow the use
> of the Elizabethan stage for the afternoon of the
> Fourth for a card of boxing matches! I assured them
> that such an event would be quite typical of the
> kind of thing that appealed to Elizabethan
> audiences.

—AS I REMEMBER. ADAM. P. 83

Cynthia Fuhrman

The Ashland Fourth of July continues as a
highpoint in the Festival calendar. Members of
the company enter the parade as "The Talent
Tomato Festival and Precision Marching Band."
William Bloodgood, Festival designer, serves
as drum major.
Left: The Festival company's winning entry in
the 1982 Fourth of July parade was a
marvelous worm.

The second part of the story is that when the receipts were counted, Shakespeare took in more than his expenses and the surplus went to cover a deficit in the prize fights!

There were several problems with the arrangements. Boxing preempted the afternoon onstage rehearsal and the fireworks went off before the arranged signal, so the last act of *Twelfth Night* was more of a triumph of pantomime than of poetry as the red, white and blue flares exploded in salute to the birth of the nation. Finally, there was a confusion about finances. The play receipts beyond expenses should have been set aside for next year's Festival and separated from the Fourth of July celebrations.

In 1936 the Festival was scheduled for August, which would give more time for rehearsal, and arrangements were made to place the receipts in the college's general fund. What could be safer than a fund replenished each year by the state legislature? Then, by an irony worthy of Sophocles, an unexpected deficit turned up in the athletic program and once again the Festival had to begin from scratch.

To head off further rivalry in the claims of actors and athletes, the Oregon Shakespearean Festival Association was incorporated in 1937. Season subscribers were made members of the association and they elected a board of directors that could guarantee the financial independence of the Festival.

The seasons that followed were ones of gradual and steady growth as the Festival settled into its characteristic repertory of four Shakespearean productions with attendance rising to about two thousand. Through his shrewd grasp of the community's traditions and his special gift in gathering a dedicated group of fellow workers and allies, Angus Bowmer succeeded in harnessing energy and enthusiasm behind his vision of what a Shakespearean Festival could be. That vision was based not only on a sophisticated understanding of how to work on the plays, but also on the special advantages of a repertory system.

It would have been easy enough to present one production a year and call it a Festival, but he was after something bigger, something that would make Ashland what the editor of the *Oregon Journal* ventured to call "the Salzburg of the West," a place that tourists might come great distances to enjoy. The Festival did not hit on the motto "Stay Four Days, See Four Plays" until sometime later, but the idea was inherent in the scheme of a four play repertory.

Repertory has advantages for actors and audiences. From the actor's point of view, the opportunity to get away from daily repetition of a single role goes a long way toward preserving spontaneity in performance. And, surprisingly, after a brief recess a performance picks up imaginative richness and color. A more important consideration is that the repertory system is in many

The Ashland Fourth of July parade, 1911.
Right: The parade in 1938.

48

ways the opposite of the star system. It places emphasis on a company, on the ensemble rather than on a star performer. It takes seriously the proverb, there are no small parts, only small actors. The king in one production may be a spear carrier in another, while doubling in one of Shakespeare's cameo roles, so-called because although brief, they are so rich in acting possibilities.

An advantage of the repertory system for audiences is that seeing an actor in a variety of roles provides a special insight and delight into the art of acting. Instead of identifying actors with a particular role, they become more sharply aware of the differences between the performers and their roles. There is a double pleasure in recognizing something that is the same only different. Perhaps that is why the casting chart showing the roles each actor takes in the repertory is a favorite feature of the souvenir program.

But the great attraction for an audience is simply the repertory itself. Long before Interstate 5 made Ashland accessible to audiences from Alaska to San Diego, Shakespearean buffs found it worthwhile to plan a trip to see four plays.

The very thought of this fair company
Clapp'd wings to me.

—HENRY VIII. 1.4.

After the Festival's fifth season Angus Bowmer took a leave of absence and William Cottrell, actor, stage manager, and director's assistant in the initial seasons, directed the repertory. One night after a performance, in the midst of the season, a fire broke out in the costume storage area. Bill Cottrell recalled how they met the crisis:

> The women in the community brought sewing machines down by the theatre, and we made costumes so there was no interruption. We did *As You Like It* in military costumes, the other costumes people ran up with amazing swiftness. The show went on... That, I think, was a great uniting thing for the people of the community.
>
> —INTERVIEW WITH NORA YEOMAN. 9/17/80

Unfortunately, a much more serious conflagration had broken out in Europe which forced the Festival to suspend operations until the end of the Second World War.

When production resumed, what had been a rather limited and local Festival was transformed into one that could claim national attention. As audiences grew so did the repertory and the number

The Festival company, wearing white gloves, cheers the 1982 Fourth of July parade from the roof of the Black Swan.

of performances. Nearly five thousand playgoers attended sixteen performances in 1947. Twenty-two years later sixty-five thousand attended sixty-five performances. The festival had become big time. It was standing room only through most of the summer and the limit had also been reached on the number of performances that could be scheduled. As long as the company was made up largely of students and teachers, rehearsals and performances had to be squeezed in between June first and Labor Day.

The repertory expanded to five productions, and all of the plays of Shakespeare were produced, not simply the better known ones that other festivals felt were all their audiences would sit still for. Ashland saw the strange tragedies *Timon of Athens* and *Titus Andronicus*, the quaint romance, *Pericles, Prince of Tyre*, and the histories, including the virtually unproduced Henry the Sixth plays. When Angus Bowmer came on stage after the opening of *Troilus and Cressida* in 1958 to announce that as of that evening the Festival had produced the canon of Shakespeare's plays, instantaneous applause broke out in the crowded theatre. He asked those who had seen them all to rise because he wished to acknowledge their contribution to that achievement. Nearly a hundred did.

Much of the Festival's amazing growth in the postwar years is a tribute to the consistent improvement in the quality of the productions, and this in turn to the people whom Angus Bowmer was able to recruit. At first they came from Stanford University, where Angus had gone for graduate study under the G.I. Bill.

Certainly the most immediate impact was made by Dr. Margery Bailey of Stanford who came to Ashland in 1948 and joined the staff as academic advisor. She was a demanding teacher, an utterly convincing actress, and she had a mind and imagination that could see the work of Shakespeare in the broad context of her own interests in the theatre, Renaissance culture and custom, folksong and story, creative writing, and English literature of the Restoration and Eighteenth Century. Her critiques of each season's repertory were challenging, personal, and unsparing. In her report of the 1949 season — thirty-two pages, single spaced — she wrote of her own performance as the nurse in *Romeo and Juliet:*

> The interpretation of the old peasant as coarse and stupidly faithful was evident in the grasp of innuendo, the complacent familiarity of the established servant, the guffaws, nudgings, and rough waddling walk . . . Miss Bailey's comic timing is dependably sound, but she cannot control the rapidity of her natural speech. The Nurse spoke in a melange of broad vowels and clipped phrasing which was as

Dr. Margery Bailey delivering her famous lecture on the Renaissance man to the Festival company.
Overleaf: A backstage tour group crosses the Elizabethan stage.

untrue to the part as the Irish brogue affected by other players.

In contrast, Myna Brunton Hughes, reviewing the production in the *Ashland Daily Tidings* awarded "first laurels" to Dr. Bailey, "for her earthy and exactly right portrayal of Angelica, nurse to Juliet. In a costume of excellent amplitude, every inflection, every gesture was the bawdy, robust, loquacious old nurse to the life."

In later years Dr. Bailey's critiques were given at staff meetings held near the end of the season. Enthroned in the Bowmers' living room, she talked while knitting string into leggings, sleeves, and hoods that when dyed and silvered made a stageworthy substitute for chain mail. With needles clicking, looking for all the world like Madame Defarge, she ran through a point by point analysis of the strengths and failings of the productions. She wanted the Festival to be better and to her that meant being faithful to the spirit of the plays as she had come to understand them. She was frankly indifferent to its growth measured by the number of productions, performances, or patrons. Despite her judgmental manner, she was very good company and eager in pursuit of the pleasures of the theatre. Lenore Glen Offord, reviewer for the *Ashland Daily Tidings* in the fifties, described Dr. Bailey in one telling sentence:

> She was one of those people that if you could please her, if you could make her respect what you were doing, you felt as if you had been knighted.
>
> —INTERVIEW WITH KAY ATWOOD 8/1/77

Her contributions to the Festival went beyond bracing criticism. Her lecture to a newly assembled company on "The Renaissance Man" was a masterpiece of informative and entertaining detail. She helped organize the Tudor Guild. In an ambitious program which she called "The Institute of Renaissance Studies," she developed courses based on the plays, published an annual gathering of writings related to the season's repertory, initiated a public lecture series, and assembled a valuable library of Renaissance books and visual materials as well as modern studies related to the context of Elizabethan drama and the interpretation of Shakespeare. Today the Margery Bailey Collection is housed at Southern Oregon State College and its development has become a continuing project of the Friends of the Library. It now includes three special treasures: the great seventeenth century folios of Jonson, Shakespeare, and Beaumont and Fletcher.

Dr. Bailey died in the spring of 1963, leaving a staff and a company sharply aware of the insights that good scholarship could bring to the production of Shakespearean drama.

One person who joined the Festival staff after the war who matched Dr. Bailey in fervor was William Patton, although it would be hard to imagine anyone more sharply contrasted in manner. In a modest, tactful way, his administrative leadership has influenced the Festival's development most profoundly.

He spent his summer vacations from Stanford working on lights, acting on occasion, and doing almost anything that had to be done. In 1953 he was appointed the Festival's first general manager and its first year-round employee. Although his position is now more accurately listed as executive director, his supervision covers the same ground as when he was taken on to do everything — handle correspondence and publicity and the box office, look to the maintenance and storage of property, solicit volunteers and donations, prepare the budget, negotiate purchases, insurance, and represent the Festival to government officials and the business community. But he did not select the plays, appoint the directors, recruit the actors, nor cast the parts. These were the responsibilities of the producing director.

Bill Patton sees his guardianship of the Festival's resources in the broadest terms. Before the popular backstage tours were regularly scheduled, a number of casual visitors dropped in backstage to wander about the hazardous area while work was going on. Finally, exasperated by the intrusions, an irate stage manager hammered an improvised sign to the entry, "Visitors are not Welcome." As soon as Bill saw it he pointed out that it was inappropriate. Our visitors, he said, are a resource we can't afford to alienate by a hasty disregard of their feelings. The sign had to come down. Not long after, he had a neatly painted sign put up pointing out that insurance regulations did not permit unauthorized persons backstage. Following this the idea of scheduled tours appeared on the staff agenda. Tours were begun and have become a regular Festival feature. Interestingly, charging a small fee so that the tour guides might get a trifle for their time found attendance more than doubling.

The story does not simply illustrate Bill Patton's ability to turn a seeming problem to mutual advantage, it also illustrates his genuine diplomatic skill, an ability to discover the point of view of everyone concerned while keeping in mind the best interests of the Festival.

Dr. Bailey did not always see that virtue in him. At such times the salutation on her communiques declined from the familiar, "Dear Lamb," past the formal, "Dear Mr. Patton," to the curt word, "General." He was moved to fire back a note headed, "Bailey." It was unfortunate, but perhaps inevitable that the high value she placed on the production as a practical way to study

Shakespeare's Renaissance world would at times be at odds with the practicalities of theatre management.

But in this Dr. Bailey was exceptional. Considering the volatile and emotional temperament on which a theatre thrives, it is to Bill Patton's credit that the Festival staff has had remarkable continuity, and although there have been serious disagreements on several occasions, seldom have disruptive squabbles erupted between the staff and the board of directors.

Of course the administration and development of a theatre's resources involves more than a diplomatic attention to personnel, or keeping track of where the money goes and where it comes from—all of which Bill Patton does in exemplary fashion. There is also the larger community that must be looked to because it affects the theatre's ability to improve. In this larger area of imaginative management he has been most active. He served as chairman of the Mt. Ashland Development Committee, the group that made Ashland a winter ski resort, partially because he likes to ski, but more importantly because the development served the interests of motels and restaurants that grew up with the Festival and needed more than a summer season to survive.

In the 1960s the Festival's situation was uncomfortable and growing untenable. The summer season was regularly sold out, which put a lid on box office receipts. At the same time an inflation rate of ten percent was eroding what the money could buy. There were two ways to reduce the pressure: cut back on production, or build an indoor theatre and expand the season. As far as Angus Bowmer and Bill Patton were concerned, cuts were out. They had spent too much time searching for ways to expand. Ready or not, the time had come to establish a spring repertory season in Ashland. The Festival had a good name and was of considerable economic value to the community, but much work had to be done before feasible proposals could be presented. It fell to Bill Patton to marshal the facts. The work was complex, but completed with amazing rapidity.

In 1966, Alfred S. V. Carpenter, a very generous patron of the Festival and chairman of the capital campaign that financed the building of the new Elizabethan stage in 1959, agreed once again to serve as general chairman of a fund drive to build an indoor complex which came to be named after the Festival's founder. A year later a report by economists from the Bureau of Business and Economic Research of the University of Oregon documented the financial peril of the Festival and its importance to the economy of Southern Oregon. The City of Ashland, acting on these findings, applied for a matching grant from the Economic Development Administration of the Department of Commerce, using the proposed theatre as the keystone of a project for downtown improvement and restoration. As construction began on the new theatre, there were obstructions and tensions in the Ashland community which at times threatened the entire project; however the federal grant was approved and everything fell into place. The theatre was dedicated on March 21, 1970 inaugurating a spring repertory of contemporary theatre. The Festival and the city had taken a big step forward. Only a theatre manager with Bill Patton's sensitivity toward his co-workers and to the larger community to which a theatre must be related could have coordinated and integrated such an expansion.

The "bricks," the open area surrounded by the Festival theatres, is often the scene of informal conversation and entertainment. Here the Black Cygnets—a group of young actors from the company and community—perform *The Deluge* as part of the festivities for the opening of the summer season in 1982. Right: William Patton, Executive Director.

TWELFTH NIGHT

Left: Wayne Ballantyne as Sir Toby; Lawrence
Paulsen, Sir Andrew; Linda Alper, Viola;
Stuart Duckworth, Fabian in *Twelfth Night*,
1981.
Below: Hugh Evans as
Sir Andrew, 1964.
Right: Raye Birk as Malvolio, 1969.
Overleaf: Juliet Randall, Olivia, and Philip
Hanson, Malvolio, 1959.
Photo Credit: Dwaine Smith

Dwaine Smith

Carolyn Mason Jones

George Francis Smith as Malvolio, 1937.
Left: Sam Pond as Feste and Joan Stuart-Morris as Olivia, 1981.
Right: The reunion of Viola (Elizabeth Huddle) and Sebastian (George Ebey), 1964.

James Carpenter as Barnardo in *Hamlet*, 1983.
Left: Mark Murphey as Hamlet, 1983.
Right: Angus Bowmer as Hamlet, 1938.

Hank Kranzler

Festival archive

Moran–Arbuckle

Claude Woolman as Hamlet and George
Peppard as Horatio, 1954.
Left: The play scene in *Hamlet*, 1954, Angus
Bowmer, director.
Right: Richard Risso as Hamlet and Ann
Kinsolving as Gertrude, 1968.
Overleaf: The duel in *Hamlet*, 1983, Robert
Benedetti, director.
Photo Credit: Hank Kranzler

Whitland Locke

Whitland Locke

The duel in *Hamlet,* 1968, Patrick Hines,
director.
Left: Claudius (Michael Kevin) interrupts
the play within the play, 1974, Jerry Turner,
director.

Dwaine Smith

Fluellen (James Smith) forces Pistol (Charles
Taylor) to eat a leek. *Henry the Fifth*, 1963.
Left: Henry receives the French ambassador.
Henry the Fifth, 1963, Jerry Turner, director.
Right: Battle sequence, *Henry the Fifth*, 1982.
Pat Patton, director.

Hank Kranzler

Hank Kranzler

Dwaine Smith

The siege of Harfleur. Powers Boothe as Henry, 1973.
Left: Stacey Keach as Henry, 1963.
Right: Henry receives the French ambassador, 1982, Pat Patton, director.
Overleaf: Stage and auditorium of the Angus Bowmer Theatre. The curtain call for *The Comedy of Errors*, 1976.
Photo Credit: Hank Kranzler

74

Richard Hay, another young man from Stanford who found his way to Ashland after the war, first came as a lighting assistant and, according to the custom of those times, to do anything else that had to be done. In 1953, after two seasons, he was named designer and technical director. Except for a handful of seasons devoted to study or to work in other theatres, he has been designing for the Festival ever since. He may well be the only person who ever designed productions for all of Shakespeare's plays.

As the designer of the Festival's three theatres and many of its productions, as well as advisor on innumerable details that call for a designer's eye, Dick Hay has had more influence than anyone on the visual style of the Festival.

The exacting standards he applies to the smallest problem are legendary. In the midst of this creative process his glasses creep downward on the nose, one hand tugs at the sideburns, as if untangling the ideas jostling for attention, while the other doodles, sketching in free, telling strokes.

During the summers of the fifties he served as both technical director and designer. He followed performances from the rear of the house, watching the technical aspects of the performance—lights, curtain cues, special effects—and the audience too, for it was important to get the feel of how they were following the play. He stayed near the phone, keeping contact with the stage manager backstage. If the wind in the trees raised the noise level, there would be a call. "Hay here. When you have a moment, get word to the company we're having a problem hearing."

There's a bizarre version of that routine that came the night a forest fire was burning on the hills to the west of Ashland. The audience, assured that ample notice would be given if the blaze took a turn toward the town, settled back to watch *Antony and Cleopatra*. As night darkened, the glow of the fire reflected on the legendary lovers. The light on the phone came on. "Yes?" "Hay here. Uh, would you tell the actors we're having trouble hearing over the roar of the flames!"

The fire was brought to heel by the time the memorable performance came to a close. The relief was indescribable, for that was the season the new Elizabethan stage was being used for the first time. What if that glorious structure, fresh with the aroma of new lumber ... the thought could not be allowed to run its course. The show must go on.

Two Gentlemen of Verona, 1974, set design by
Richard Hay.

78

The old Elizabethan stage, rebuilt in the Chautauqua shell when productions resumed after the war, was a simple two-story facade. Concealed behind was a crowded backstage, a labyrinth of corridors, dressing rooms, shops and storage areas. In the early fifties there were discussions about rebuilding on a grander scale and in a design reflecting current notions about the appearance of an Elizabethan stage. These speculations came to a halt in 1958 when the fire inspector ruled that the structure was unsafe and had to be replaced. For the new building, Dick Hay specified the technical requirements and developed the design in collaboration with the architect, Jack Edson of Medford. Together they consciously copied the overall dimensions of the Fortune Theatre, built in 1600 by the contractor who constructed Shakespeare's theatre.

The new theatre is a marvelous and ingenious achievement. It towers more than twice as high as its predecessor, embracing an auditorium set at a deeper pitch to focus the audience more perfectly toward the stage. The Tudor half-timber decorative details give way to plainer surfaces in the main playing area so as not to draw attention from the costumed actor. Within and behind the theatrical facade, from the flying machine in the penthouse to the trap elevators beneath the stage, are complex modern electrical and mechanical devices. Some of them are standard theatre equipment, but many are inventions and adaptations which only a technical director experienced in Ashland productions could have anticipated.

Within ten years the Festival's need for an extended season made it urgent that an indoor theatre be built. Dick Hay was called upon to develop the design and theatrical requirements for the new theatre, this time as consultant to the Seattle architectural firm of Kirk, Wallace and McKinley. In providing an indoor theatre that would serve for the classical and modern as well as the Shakespearean repertory, the open-stage form was adopted. The important feature of this form is that stage and auditorium are not treated as separate spaces; they merge into one. The audience appears to enclose the open stage, sharing the same space as the actors.

The peculiar problems posed by this form have hardly been more beautifully resolved than by Hay's design for the large indoor theatre. The theatre seats six hundred, yet the sense of an intimate, immediate relationship to the stage is dominant. In a crowded house, the place is alive with a special vitality. Nowhere else are audiences so often moved to rise for applause at a curtain call. Their involvement owes much to the simple and harmonious relationship of stage and auditorium.

A third theatre was added to the Festival's complex in 1977. It was called the Black Swan, to suggest the experimental and

The Elizabethan stage designed by Richard L. Hay. Full cast on stage for opening of *Henry the Fifth*, 1973, Laird Williamson, director.

eccentric dramatic fare it was designed to house. It is a converted automobile showroom, not a new theatre building. Dick Hay and R. Duncan MacKenzie, then the Festival's technical director, collaborated in planning and supervising the conversion. The theatre is a simple rectangular "black box" with an overhead lighting grid and flexible seating, so that the playing space can be arranged in a variety of configurations to fit individual productions. The lobby walls are faced with a diagonal patchwork of mirrors which has the effect of preparing members of the audience for the inescapable view of their fellows in the seats opposite them. More importantly, the mirrors suggest that a theatre is a place where they may glimpse variations of themselves as the play unfolds.

Dick Hay has created the Festival's visual style not only in the stages he developed for its use, but in the wealth of fresh and intriguing designs he developed for productions in the three theatres. There is a noticeable restraint in a Hay design, a masterful use of color, scale, perspective and proportion controlled by an evident delight in understatement. His forms might seem very classic and formal were it not for the quality of movement that he brings into play.

This quality can be seen in the elegant design for the 1974 production of *Two Gentlemen of Verona* where sweeping, romantic curves and merry circles set the stage dancing with the actors. Sometimes there is movement in a more literal sense, as in the modern *Julius Caesar,* presented in 1982. There, a tall colonnade, pretentious and overreaching as Caesar himself, would slowly sink downward during the intermission and in the course of the action, setting the stage for the final battle.

Movement is not arbitrarily introduced. It comes naturally out of the movement and meaning of the play as the director interprets it. The design derives its point from the live performance. As Dick Hay expresses the matter:

> Any idea a scene designer has is only as good as its enhancement of the director's goals and intentions. It has no significance outside the event of the performance.
>
> —QUOTED IN TATE, *A SPACE FOR MAGIC.* P.6

The words express at once his personality and his credo. He is there to serve the performance.

Hank Kranzler

The Black Swan before a rehearsal.
Right: *Julius Caesar,* 1982, set design by Richard L. Hay. Brutus (Philip Davidson) stands by the body of Caesar as Antony (Barry Kraft) approaches for the famous oration.
Far right: Richard L. Hay.

*I have liv'd
To see inherited my very wishes
And the buildings of my fancy;*

—CORIOLANUS. 2.1.

There were many others who joined the Festival company after the Second World War and contributed to its growth and the quality of its productions. The most active of the directors in the fifties was James Sandoe who came from the University of Colorado, a sprightly man whose energy was as inexhaustible as his wit. After rehearsals he sat late at the typewriter working up notes—wide ranging, personal and perceptive—to each member of his cast.

Jim Sandoe had the utmost confidence in Shakespeare. He sneered at directors who thought "they had to help Willie along." He did the plays straight and uncut. And he proved his point in guiding the company through the *terra incognita* of the Henry the Sixth plays. He was the first to tackle *Troilus and Cressida*, and if he didn't exactly win that one, he wasn't bruised in the scrimmage either. It was pretty much at his insistence that the Festival introduced the work of other Elizabethan playwrights with his production of Webster's *Duchess of Malfi* in 1960.

The directorial and technical staff of the summer Festival was a relatively stable group. In addition to Jim Sandoe, there were Allen Fletcher, Robert Loper and Richard Risso who regularly joined Angus Bowmer on the directorial staff, as did Jerry Turner who succeeded Angus as the Festival's producing director in 1971. On the technical staff, Douglas Russell, and later Marie Chesley, designed and supervised construction of costumes. Hugh Evans designed lighting and later directed. Bernard Windt was director of music, Shirlee Dodge, choreographer, and Carl Ritchie, public relations director.

Most of the staff were actors as well, although they could not take on much more than one role a year. An exception was Richard Graham, an accomplished actor from New York. He wanted the experience of working in Shakespeare and came to Ashland in 1948—the only Shakespearean Festival in North America at the time, for the San Diego Festival did not resume postwar production until a year later.

Dick Graham acted with the company for twelve seasons and managed to work on productions of all Shakespeare's plays. He directed five, but acting was the center of his work. He did the giant roles of Lear and Othello in several stagings, and a wealth of fine characterizations. With a splendid voice, he could make the most complicated passages come alive with meaning, and no one was better at showing off a costume. His performances and exam-

James Sandoe

84

Richard Graham as King Lear, 1951.
Left: The Vining Theatre, Ashland, 1914,
later called the Lithia.

ple did much to strengthen the company. His staff work included editing the souvenir program and supervising make-up.

Another staff member was Gertrude Bowmer. Officially she was secretary to her husband, the producing director, but her interest in things theatrical ran too deep for her work to stop at correspondence and the appointment calendar. She followed every production closely, attended nearly every performance, knew and remembered everyone in the growing company.

The Bowmer correspondence was a hefty piece of work by itself for the acting company was selected through applications sent in by mail rather than by audition. Later, the Bowmers were able to travel to interview prospective actors at some of the larger drama and theatre departments, but these excursions did more to stimulate additional applications than simplify selection of the company.

At staff meetings Mrs. Bowmer seldom spoke. When she did her quick, dry, thoroughly Oregonian wit was an exact complement to her husband's zestful ebullience.

As long as the Festival was a summer affair, its acting company was largely drawn from the ranks of students and teachers in schools like the University of Texas, Stanford, Carnegie Tech, and smaller colleges as near as Reed and as far away as Franklin and Marshall in Pennsylvania. They met in June, rehearsed in July, performed in August and dispersed in September. They necessarily had divergent and contradictory attitudes about acting in general and rather awkward notions about acting Shakespeare in particular.

If Angus Bowmer and the veterans he was able to persuade to return were in the directorial chairs, they were unable to develop ensemble work in the short time available for rehearsals. Dash and excitement were there, but not always well channeled. Certainly there was little chance for sustained development.

Angus Bowmer was well aware of this limitation and restless about it. He kept coming up with various schemes to transcend the impasse. As early as 1951 an experiment was made to see if a small winter company could be supported in Ashland. That would provide a nucleus of experienced actors to enrich the summer company. In association with Richard Graham, Angus organized the Vining Repertory Company and began a season of four contemporary plays using the Lithia Theatre, an unused legitimate theatre that had been built in Ashland in 1914. They had encouraging success until, in the midst of their second season, the theatre was destroyed by fire and the project had to be abandoned for want of a suitable indoor theatre in which to perform.

Hopes of reviving the Vining Repertory continued to occupy Bowmer's thoughts and he tried again in the early sixties using the

Varsity, Ashland's movie house, as a makeshift theatre, under the sponsorship of Southern Oregon College. The effort was too expensive to continue.

Another way of lengthening the time a company or a part of it could be kept together was to go on tour. The difficulties here were even more forbidding. The Festival board balked at his proposals on several occasions. Angus was able to accept an invitation from Dean Virgil Whitaker of Stanford to open his 1964 repertory in Frost Amphitheatre as part of the University's celebrations of the quadricentennial of Shakespeare's birth. But aside from that generously subsidized engagement, the Festival seasons were locked into a summer schedule.

Beginning in 1966, Angus experimented by using the Varsity movie house for matinee performances of ballad operas during the summer season. He succeeded in demonstrating that if an indoor theatre were available for matinees in the summer and for a spring repertory, Festival income would have a chance to keep up with inflation. That consideration, plus the fact that the Festival had become important to the economy of the area, at last made the building of a new indoor theatre an obvious step. What had seemed an impossible dream had become a solid proposition.

Getting funds and plans together was nerve-wracking work. Perhaps the most heartwarming surprise came when Julie Carpenter Daugherty, a friend of the Festival and former member of the board of the Vining Repertory, offered a substantial donation on condition that she be allowed to name the new theatre. The offer was accepted and she called Angus to tell him it would be called the Angus Bowmer Theatre.

The ceremonies attending the opening of the new theatre were held on Saturday afternoon and evening, March 21, 1970. The program proudly announced "A second stage for the Oregon Shakespearean Festival, made possible by donations from its far-reaching patrons, plus an Economic Development grant through the cooperation of the City of Ashland." This unusual combination of forces underscored the Festival's importance not only to its audience, but to the community at large.

The dedication on Saturday afternoon was at once formal and personal. Everyone was aware that something very extraordinary was happening, involving friends of long standing, and centering on that patient, indomitable showman who kept telling them the Festival could be better than they had thought possible.

Governor Tom McCall, in the formal naming of the theatre, spoke for everyone:

> The dream did not, even in the beginning, walk
> alone. There were loving hearts and talented hands
> and a legion of unnamed laborers who soon came

Bill Bayley

The Angus Bowmer Theatre, opening night, March 21, 1970.
Right: *Lock Up Your Daughters*, 1968, in the Varsity Theatre. Amanda McBroom as Hilaret and Larry Alan Haynes as Ramble.

into this story. That was a brave and daring band back in the thirties. They flourished with what some professors like to call "the valour of ignorance." They didn't know that a Shakespearean Festival in a what's-its-name town way out in a whatcha-ma-call-it state is ridiculous...

So they went on and flourished and built under the golden suns of summer a world of dreams by night. What they did has at last been appreciated. And the leader of that idea—the man who had a dream which was not all a dream—has finally been honored in perpetuity. And it's high time.

With characteristic humility Angus accepted the laurels of the day with a promise for the future. "How do I say thank you?" he asked. "What could I possibly say in response to such an honor? Our thanks will come in using the building to the fullest."

The Festival began making good on that promise that very evening with a performance of *Rosencrantz and Guildenstern are Dead* directed by Angus Bowmer. It was the first of a four-play repertory that ran for forty-three performances and drew an audience of over eighteen thousand.

And tidings do I bring, and lucky joys
And golden times and happy news of price.

—II HENRY IV. 5.3.

With the opening of the Bowmer Theatre nearly everything about the Festival changed. Immediately the number of performances tripled and attendance doubled. Ten years later the number of performances nearly tripled again and attendance more than doubled again. The Bowmer Theatre was indeed being used to the fullest. When the Black Swan opened, the repertory went from nine to twelve new productions a year in a season that ran from February through October.

Shortly after these transformations began, Angus Bowmer recognized that his health made it advisable that a new producing director be appointed to assure the future of the rapidly expanding Festival. The search for a new director proceeded rapidly and Dr. Jerry Turner was appointed in May of 1971. At the time he was professor of drama at the University of California, Riverside, but no stranger to Ashland.

A veteran of eleven seasons, Jerry Turner had directed nine productions starting in 1959 when he staged *The Maske of the New*

The sign was made from a piece of lumber, one of the first donations to the Festival.
Left: Festival musician William Adams playing a bass dulcian.
Overleaf: Richard Elmore makes up for the role of Adolphus Spanker in *London Assurance*, 1984.
Photo Credit: Jim Chrisman

91

World, a short musical extravaganza written by Carl Ritchie, with music by Bernie Windt. It was performed as a curtain raiser to performances of *Twelfth Night. The Maske* was both the Festival's salute to the Oregon Centennial and, as the opening production on the new Elizabethan stage, the occasion to display its technical resources.

Queen Elizabeth was enthroned on stage and the entertainment was presented as if by her courtiers. Dick Hay designed and engineered the special effects in the manner of a masque by Inigo Jones. There were Indian dancers, transformations and finally a vision of the new world where "in Oregon's high mountains...a shrine is raised to Elizabeth...to Shakespeare." The Queen was pleased.

If Jerry Turner's first assignment as play director in Ashland was to stage these spectacular novelties, his debut as producing director was accompanied with far less bustle and tension. For one thing, while Angus Bowmer remained active in the affairs of the Festival as development consultant, he gave a clear stage to his successor.

Angus had always believed that it was essential that a producing director have the prerogative of selecting the plays and the personnel to direct, design and perform them if his responsibilities for the artistic quality of the productions were to be fulfilled. He had no intention of going back on a point he had fought many times to maintain.

The transition also went well because Jerry Turner is very like Angus in his approach and feeling toward the theatre. He has the same generous openness to what others can contribute, the same down-to-earth distrust of the arty and highfalutin'.

Jerry enjoys talking to people and has some good stories to swap. He looks and carries himself like a rancher from his native Colorado. He once confessed in lines of free verse:

> Still, I know my best work has always had
> More beet pulp and alfalfa in it
> Than greasepaint.
> The shape of a scene has more to do
> With childhood anxieties of the Depression
> And youthful fever of World War II
> Than with the silence of libraries
> Or the sweaty pretence of rehearsal halls.
> We can only show what we know.
>
> —FESTIVAL SOUVENIR PROGRAM, '78, P. 56

But the look and the confession are deceptive. He is a careful student of drama and an eager reader of all sorts of things that relate to its background. Few directors go into rehearsal more

Festival archive

Jerry Turner, Artistic Director.
Right: The final prophecy and vision of Oregon from *The Maske of the New World*, 1959, by Carl Ritchie.

fully prepared to explore the dramatic possibilities recorded in the script. Yet few are less dogmatic, so open to new insights discovered in rehearsal, so able to elicit collaboration from a cast. In moments of disruptive laughter that would drive most directors wild, Jerry can relax and let tensions dissipate.

In guiding the Festival through a longer season and a new repertory, new policies had to be set. There are only thirty-seven plays in the accepted canon of Shakespeare's works. Neither an audience nor a company can be expected to sustain interest in a performance of *Twelfth Night* every three years even if it were set in a rocket ship one year and in Tibet the next.

Considering the urgency of increasing attendance, a producing director might be tempted to underrate his potential audience and try musical comedies or the latest Broadway hits. Jerry Turner turned in another direction, as everyone knew he would.

He is familiar with a large body of classic and contemporary drama that speak of the recurring concerns of human beings rather than of the fads and excitements of the moment. Such plays are seldom produced in the commercial theatre or even in many academic theatres. He guessed that an audience devoted to Shakespeare might be likely to welcome a chance to see them; and, further, that there was an audience that hadn't yet given Shakespeare a try which might be attracted by a group of modern plays. He was right on both counts.

Although more plays by other dramatists are now produced in Ashland, Shakespeare remains at the center of the repertory both in number of performances and in size of attendance. Occasionally someone writes a letter expressing regret that this or that contemporary drama has been mounted side by side with the many-minded Shakespeare. There is at the same time, however, a growing awareness that the ambiguity and complexity we value in modern literature is also at the heart of Shakespeare's appeal. To see him in the company of Beckett and Brecht, Strindberg and Stoppard, O'Neill and Osborne is to open both Shakespeare and them to our fuller understanding.

A company as well as an audience benefits from opportunities to explore new styles of theatre, to try things that may miss the mark. Such experiments stimulate creative energy and imagination, qualities that must be maintained at a high level if the established and familiar repertory is to be handled effectively.

Jerry Turner's proposals for the Black Swan, an alternative playing space for alternative theatre pieces, were consistent with this view of the needs of a company devoted to a classic repertory.

Exploring a variety of theatre around a Shakespearean center requires additional directorial talents. Unlike the members of the resident staff, most directors are now in Ashland only for the rehearsal period. After the opening performances, the produc-

The curtain call for *Brand*, 1976, directed by Jerry Turner.

tions are in the hands of the stage managers whose job it is to keep them running in line with the director's instructions. This allows the Festival to recruit visiting directors from theatres around the country. The company works with as many as eight or nine different directors a season, extending the range and style of the performances.

Continuity is provided by the resident staff, Jerry Turner and Pat Patton, and by several directors who have returned on a more or less regular basis. Three have been particularly active. Dennis Bigelow first came to Ashland as stage manager and began directing in 1978. In 1983 he was appointed artistic director of the Eleanor McClatchy Performing Arts Center in Sacramento. James Edmondson from Colorado, one of the Festival's most accomplished and versatile actors, first joined the company in 1972 and has doubled as actor and director rather steadily in the seasons that followed. James Moll from Texas directed *Much Ado About Nothing* in 1965. He wasn't able to return until 1976 but since then has been regularly on the staff.

The all-time record for number of productions directed is now held by Jerry Turner. He usually directs two productions a year, one Shakespeare and one modern drama — Strindberg is a personal favorite — or a play by one of the Elizabethan-Jacobean dramatists.

Running a close second to Jerry's record is Pat Patton's. Pat is now the associate director of the Festival. He began by directing *You Can't Take It With You* in the 1970 spring repertory. He was the production manager, a sort of combined general stage manager and first sergeant. Pat Patton brings to Shakespearean comedy an actor's flair for zany inventions controlled by a director's grasp of where the scene has to go. In 1984 he celebrated his twentieth year at the Festival with a richly comic staging of *The Taming of the Shrew* that was taken on a seven-week tour of California. The same season saw his powerful *Cat On a Hot Tin Roof.* Besides directing, Pat works out the meeting, rehearsal, and performance schedules which require constant checking to see that they work. Despite the rigor of clockwatching, he radiates the spirit of a master of revels. He is all over the place. There is a saying around the theatre that the best way to find him is to stay put until he comes by.

Another regular member of the staff who celebrated twenty seasons with the Festival in 1984 is Jeannie Davidson. As resident costume designer, she has produced a body of work that few can match. Jeannie began working as costume shop manager for costume designer Marie Chesley, then for Jack Byers. She was appointed designer in 1969 and has costumed over a hundred productions for the Festival. Her costumes give imaginative expression to the characters and the world in which they move. If

Hank Kranzler

Pat Patton.
Right: The witches (Anya Springer, Rex Rabold and Mary Turner) in *Macbeth*, 1979, Pat Patton, director.

Jeannie Davidson.
Left: The Festival Exhibit Center. Displays are changed periodically to illustrate Festival craftsmanship and archival material: photographs, designs, props and costumes.

the play demands realistic period costumes, she provides them down to the last detail of materials, tailoring and accessories. Bodices are laced at the back if that was the custom, even if a cape may conceal the lacings, to assure the feel and carriage of the period. If she could afford it, the crowns would all be fourteen carats fine.

Historical accuracy, however, is not the final word in a Davidson design. The costume must make its impact at the rear of a twelve-hundred seat house, and plays are seldom as realistic as they are expressive of certain mental and emotional qualities. Jeannie is an expert at modifying a style to fill these theatrical demands, and if a director asks for something strange and different, her sketches can show an unexpected wealth of fantasy.

She believes the design process cannot be complete until the plays are actually open. She watches closely through the fittings, the dress rehearsals and the opening performances, taking copious notes. Does the costume look right under the lights? What happened to the jaunty drape we wanted in the cloak? Should the hat brim be stiffened? Indeed, the work is never done until the audience sees what she imagined. Then the process begins again with sketches for next season's repertory.

A relative newcomer to the regular staff is scenic designer William Bloodgood, who began designing at Ashland in 1976. Since then Bill and Dick Hay have more or less divided productions between them. Although there are differences in their work, they share the same meticulous attention to detail and the same views of the function of design in the theatre. Bill expressed his views in this way:

> I am alternately frustrated and immensely excited by this work. We manufacture imitations of realities — shaky facades that fade with time or are chopped up for firewood. And yet, as one production comes down we are already preparing for the next, always expecting it to be even better than its precursor. We seem never to stop. My role as a scene designer... is to create spaces in which actors may perform and characters may live.
>
> —FESTIVAL SOUVENIR PROGRAM, '78, P. 54.

Almost nightly at the Tudor Fair, an entertainment that precedes the theatrical fare, standing outside the crowd by the dance platform, watching intently is the choreographer, Judith Kennedy. She practically grew up with the Festival. Her parents took her to see Jim Sandoe's 1950 production of *Antony and Cleopatra* when she was six, supposing that she would fall asleep. She remembers it as the night she "fell in love with the Festival."

Later she played a fairy in *A Midsummer Night's Dream* and one of the princes murdered in the Tower by that royal scoundrel, Richard the Third. Through high school and college she danced at the Fair while working in the costume shop.

After graduate studies in dance at Mills College and numerous workshops along the way, she became expert in modern and Renaissance dance forms. Since 1971 she has been the Festival's resident choreographer for the Tudor Fair, the summer dance concerts, and for most of the dance sequences in the plays.

Judy is but one of many in the company whose life took its direction from early experiences in the theatre. The acting company is a diverse group. Which means that generalizations about its members don't hold up, except the obvious one that they are individuals. They come from the east and south as well as the west. They are young in spirit, although older and more experienced than the actors who gathered in Ashland in the days of the summer Festivals. Nearly all of them have completed graduate study in theatre and many have tried working in other fields — teaching, sales, or preparing for quite different careers — before recognizing that the theatre was their calling.

However different their training and experience have been — theatre training programs in universities and studios could hardly be described as standardized—one generalization will hold: The Ashland actors are no longer initiates on trial; they are confirmed professionals, disciplined and devoted to their work. It is, as they say, their life.

Though some were in college before they were introduced to the irresistible theatre, for most it happened when they were quite young. They remember those experiences with gratitude.

Recognizing the need to develop young audiences, since television cannot replace the live actor in awakening a love of theatre and literature, the Festival began a program addressed to school children.

Forbes Rogers, a teacher and actor, was appointed education coordinator in 1970. Classroom materials were developed, teams of actors began visiting schools, workshops for teachers and students were scheduled, and school groups began coming to Ashland to attend the plays and participate in discussions with members of the company. He and Homer Swander, then director of the Festival's Institute of Renaissance Studies, developed and encouraged other new programs for students and teachers, including the popular actor visits to the schools.

More recently, the Festival's Information and Education Office headed by Peggy Rubin with Paul Barnes as education coordinator, has enlarged this outreach to schools: In 1984, for example, eight teams of two actors visited classrooms, held workshops and assembly programs in two hundred and sixty schools in California,

Judith Kennedy

Stage manager Kimberley Jean Barry in the
control booth of the Angus Bowmer Theatre.
Right: The Festival production staff meets
weekly under a soft sculpture bust of
Shakespeare.

Oregon, Washington, Alaska, Idaho, Nevada, and British Columbia. Total attendance ran to one hundred and forty-five thousand.

The response to these programs has been unexpectedly heart-warming and stimulating for the actors as well as the students. Mimi Carr tells of trying the scene where Richard the Third offers his sword to Lady Anne, challenging her to kill him or accept his hand in marriage. Mimi and another actress were visiting a class in what was described as a tough neighborhood. Would the students accept a woman in a man's role? Would they grasp the situation? Lady Anne took the sword. She hesitated. In the tense classroom a girl's voice was heard: "Kill him."

A young boy in one of the California schools wrote:

> Dear Ashland players
> I'm writing to thank you for the play. My favorite part was the sword fighting. I practice sword fighting a lot at home.

While they all seem to remember the swords, another student concluded a longer letter by writing: "I hope you can come back soon. The language was great too. I loved it."

Acting in Ashland has many rewards. The opportunity to play a long season in a varied repertory is something no other theatre can offer. The typical hassle of an actor's life — looking for work, moving about for a short engagement and moving again—can be set aside for a year. In many cases actors take up residency in Ashland for a short term, then return again for a longer one, and some become permanent residents of the town that is growing ever more stimulating to actors, both in terms of their professional and personal needs.

Although Angus Bowmer and his colleagues may be credited with many sterling qualities, it is unlikely that they, singularly or collectively, could have predicted the growth of a Fourth of July event which shared billing with boxing matches, a parade, and some ill-timed fireworks, into the hardy institution the Festival has become. One can only imagine the pride felt by Bowmer as he watched the Festival's physical facilities grow to three state-of-the-art stages and attendance swell to almost a quarter-million.

Festival actor Hugh Hastings works with a student group, 1983.
Left: An eager crowd waits for the doors of the Bowmer Theatre to open for a student matinee.

Cynthia Fuhrman

105

His life was gentle, and the elements
So mix'd in him that Nature might stand up
And say to all the world, "This was a man!"

—JULIUS CAESAR. 5.5

Angus Bowmer died on May 26, 1979, in his seventy-fourth year. Ten days later a "Festival Salute" in his honor was given in the theatre named after him.

The crowded house sat silently. Then they heard, as if from a great distance, the sound of a bagpipe. More pipers joined in. Slowly they moved from the lobby into the auditorium, wearing full clan dress, down the right aisle and onto the stage. A long line across the stage. Their solemn sound continuing there. And on out the left aisle. Gradually the skirl faded in the distance. Silence again.

This unforgettable tribute was paid by the Southern Oregon Kilty Band. Year by year at the "Feast of the Tribe of Will," which is held at the opening of the summer season, the Kilty Band had piped for the Gathering of the Clan, serenaded the guests and piped them into the outdoor theatre. They had come back at the turning of the year, telling of the rich heritage that Angus had left to the tribe.

Perhaps Jerry Turner put it in words as nearly as anyone can when he said:

> The theatre's a place where, in Thornton Wilder's
> words, people can show most vividly what it's like
> to be a human being. That doesn't seem like much,
> sometimes, but Angus Bowmer showed us in his
> life and in his work, that it's everything.

—FESTIVAL SOUVENIR PROGRAM, '79, P. 40

Festival archive

The Southern Oregon Kilty Band entertains at the Feast of the Tribe of Will, 1979. Right: *Much Ado About Nothing*, 1976, James Edmondson, director.

106

I delight in masques and revels sometimes altogether.
—TWELFTH NIGHT. 1.3

Summer evenings, audiences gather in Ashland nearly an hour before performance time to enjoy the Tudor Fair. It is a gallimaufry of dancing and singing and playing on the recorders and other early instruments, with occasional jigs and juggling, by the Festival musicians and dancers. Meanwhile the refreshment stands are open and the peddlers and program hawkers mingle with the crowd. The atmosphere is bright and carefree. First-time patrons drink in the entertainment, waiting expectantly for the play to begin. Veteran playgoers settle casually into their seats and examine their programs for familiar names, adjusting their lap robes if outdoors and facing the cooling evening. The neophytes will be pleased, even excited, by the quality of the production; the veterans knowing, yet expectant. They are accustomed to professionalism at the Festival.

The punctuality of the clocklike beginnings of the plays in the three discrete theatres, the beauty and detail of the costumes, the utilitarian yet aesthetic nature of props and scenery, and the splendid performances of the actors have become hallmarks of the Festival. The Festival represents the best in regional theatre, and regional theatre may represent the best in theatre.

The nearly two thousand playgoers who cross the courtyard each summer evening, filling the twelve hundred seat Elizabethan Theatre and the six hundred seat Angus Bowmer Theatre, represent a fraction of the three hundred thousand viewers who enjoy the Festival's over six hundred performances during the season. The cultural impact the Festival has on the entire Pacific Coast comes into focus when one learns that ninety percent of the audience lives more than one hundred and fifty miles from Ashland. Nearly twenty percent of the patrons originate from the San Francisco Bay Area, twenty percent from the Portland area, with patrons from the Seattle, Sacramento, and Oregon's Willamette Valley areas each comprising just under ten percent of the audience.

Visitors from beyond the Rogue Valley have not only made Ashland a cultural center, they have also made it a center of the tourist industry in Oregon. It is estimated that the Festival attracts visitors to the Rogue Valley whose economic impact is over fifty million dollars annually. This amount takes on greater significance when the growing attendance figures are contrasted with the roller-coaster performance of the lumber-dependent economy of the state. The Festival's budget, covered through ticket sales, education programs, concessions, and gifts and grants, makes the company both financially stable and the source of envy of comparable theatres in the nation.

Like the notion of a five million dollar budget amounting to a fifty million dollar economic benefit to the Ashland area, it is difficult to grasp the cultural influence of the Festival. One yardstick could be that of a small-college drama teacher, say Angus Bowmer, who in a teaching lifetime of thirty years might expose, generously, ten thousand students to classical drama. The theatre has played to over four million during its history and the Festival's Outreach Program has played to over one million.

This endeavor speaks to the Festival's concern for maintaining a vital audience, for, according to the Festival's mission statement:

> It is our intention to bring the classical theatre out of the library and into the living consciousness of the modern playgoer. We intend to provide a theatrical bridge between our cultural heritage and modern experience.

The statement continues:

> Our major task is to select and perform plays of dramatic stature, whether ancient or contemporary, classical or modern, which speak to the human condition, and to present them as vividly and as clearly and as boldly as our resources permit, making demands on our audiences as well as ourselves in the pursuit of an ideal which, by its nature, will never be achieved: the definitive production.

Pursuit of that elusive ideal has animated the Festival's history. From its beginnings the Festival has grown in every respect: number of plays presented, audience size, and critical acclaim. Complacency is unwelcome at the Festival: What was done well can be improved upon.

1983 was the Festival's vintage year for awards to date. In that year it became the only theatre in the country to receive a National Governors' Association award for distinguished service to the arts; and the nation's highest theatre award, the Tony.

Tony Awards are given annually by the League of New York Theatres and Producers in honor of the late Antoinette Perry of the American Theatre Wing for "distinguished achievement" in Broadway theatres. The awards were established in 1947. More recently the American Theatre Critics Association has been assigned to nominate regional theatres outside New York for "distinguished theatre" awards for achievement over a period of years.

Jerry Turner and William Patton journeyed to New York to accept the citation and silver medallion at the formal celebrations.

Jerry remembers an incidental encounter that to him was as much a stamp of approval as the Tony itself:

> We didn't feel like getting on the subway in broad daylight dressed in our rented tuxedos, so we walked from our hotel. There was time to stop for a drink beforehand, and the first thing our waitress said to us was, "Are you the musicians?" We told her no, actually we were there for the Tony Awards that were being given out next door.
>
> "No kidding?" she said. "Right next door and I didn't even know it was tonight! I'll bet you'd like to know who the winners are." As a matter of fact, we told her, we already won an award. "No kidding!" she said. "You mean that stuff about it being a surprise is all made up?" We told her ours was special and so we knew ahead of time.
>
> "No kidding! Where you from?" As soon as we said Oregon, she yelled "No kidding! You know, I was in Ashland once and saw one of the Shakespeare plays. It was the best acting I had ever seen in my life. That's when I decided to become an actress. In fact, that's why I'm in New York now."
>
> She started to make her exit, then checked herself for a second. "Hey, what was your order?" After that it didn't seem to matter much what we ordered.

When the Festival first learned of the Tony, Jerry wrote to the company. His letter concluded with these words:

> Our theatre was founded and nurtured not to win prizes, however pleasant and rewarding they are, but in the certain knowledge that by cultivating an art of illusion, we might arrive at something like a Truth. The Antoinette Perry Award is testament to our achievement, past and present, and it is a pleasure to share it with Angus and Gertrude Bowmer and the hundreds who have worked in Ashland over the years. But it is also permanently true that:
>
> *What's past is prologue; what to come,*
> *In yours and my discharge.*

A FESTIVAL CHRONOLOGY

We see which way the stream of time doth run.

—II HENRY IV. 4.1

1935—Elizabethan stage built in Chautauqua shell.
First Annual Shakespearean Festival opens July 2nd.

1937—Festival Association incorporated.

1940—Costume stock nearly destroyed by fire.

1941-1946—Festival closed during World War II.

1947—Second Elizabethan stage built.
Festival resumes production.

1948—Tudor Guild organized.
Dr. Margery Bailey appointed Academic Advisor.

1951—Festival attendance tops 10,000.

1953—William Patton appointed General Manager.
Richard Hay appointed Designer and Technical Director.

1959—New Elizabethan stage built.

1960—*The Duchess of Malfi*, first non-Shakespearean play, is produced.

1963—Attendance tops 50,000.

1964—Festival tours three productions to Stanford University.

1966—Festival uses Varsity Movie Theatre to stage ballad operas.

1970—Angus Bowmer Theatre opens March 21st.
Festival Education office established.

1971—Jerry Turner appointed Producing Director of Festival.
Attendance tops 150,000.

1975—Festival Exhibit Center opens.

1977—Black Swan opens February 11th.

1978—Development office established.

1982—Two-week tour of *Comedy of Errors* through Washington.

1983—Festival wins Tony and National Governors' Association Awards.
Attendance tops 300,000.

1984—Festival welcomes four millionth visitor.
Seven-week tour of *The Taming of the Shrew* through California.

1985—Festival celebrates its 50th Anniversary.

1935

2⁰⁰

THE CITY OF ASHLAND
—PRESENTS—

The First Annual Shakespearean Festival

Under the Direction of
ANGUS L. BOWMER

"TWELFTH NIGHT"
Tuesday and Thursday, 8 P. M.

The Persons of the Play—

Sebastian, brother to Viola .... Dolph Janes
Antonio, friend to Sebastian .... Merrill Gunter
Sea Captain, friend to Viola .... Jim Foster
Valentine) Attendants to .... Helen Ellenberger
Curio) Duke .... Beth Cummings
Orsino, duke of Illyria .... Marion Frost
Sir Toby Belch, uncle to Olivia .. Angus L. Bowmer
Sir Andrew Aguecheek .... John Barker
Malvolio, steward to Olivia .... Geo. F. Smith
Fabian) Servants to .... Bill Eberhart
(Feste, a clown) Olivia .... Robert Stedman
Olivia, a rich countess .... Dorothy Pruitt
Viola, in love with Orsino .... Jeanne Daugherty
Maria, Olivia's woman .... Jeanne Fabrick
Priest .... Tom Palmer
Officer .... Bill Cottrell

Scene: A city in Illyria and the Sea coast near it.

PRODUCTION STAFF

Costumes designed by .... Lois M. Bowmer
Construction Manager .... R. Berry
Wardrobe Mistresses
.... Maxine Gearhart, Billie Brandes
.... Jeanne Fabrick
Properties .... Tom Palmer
Electrician .... Noma Weaver
Book Holder .... Marion Ady, Angus Bowmer
Make-up .... Gordon MacCracken
Publicity

Music orchestrated and directed by Lawrence Hubert

ORCHESTRA PERSONNEL

Violins

Mary Roberson
Alicia Coggins
Florence Hubert
Leslie Kincaid
Viola
Andrew Johnson
Cello
Phyllis Sparr

Frances Aikens
Ruth Hardy
Laverne Roberson
Jean Billings
Flute
Lorraine Sparr
Piano
Flossie Thompson
Reeds
Rosa Franko

"MERCHANT OF VENICE"
Wednesday at 8 P. M.

The Persons of the Play—

Duke of Venice .... Marion Frost
Prince of Morocco) Suitors to .... John Harr
Prince of Arragon) Portia .... Karl Moore
Antonio, a Merchant of Venice .... Ed. Butze
Bassanio, his friend .... Robert Stedman
Gratiano) Friends to ...... Geo. F. Smith
Salanio) Antonio and .... Merrill Gunter
Salarino) Bassanio .... Tom Palmer
Lorenzo, in love with Jessica .... Jim Foster
Shylock, a rich Jew .... Angus L. Bowmer
Launcelot Gobbo .... John Chipley
A servant to Shylock
Old Gobbo, father to Launcelot .... Bill Cottrell
Leonardo, servant to Bassanio .. Helen Ellenberger
Stephano, servant to Portia .... Beth Cummings
Tubal, friend to Shylock .... Bill Cottrell
Portia, a rich heiress .... Helen Edmiston
Nerissa, her waiting maid .... Beverly Young
Jessica, daughter to Shylock .... Wanada Aldrich
Curtain boys .... Audrey Lofland, Wilma Copple
Magnificoes and other attendants: Bob Root,
Maxine Gearhart, Vernon Clark, Jack Sanderson,
Don Darnielle.
Scene: Partly at Venice and partly at Belmont,
the seat of Portia, on the continent.

THE REPERTORY 1935-1985

1935

The Merchant of Venice
Twelfth Night
   Angus Bowmer, Director
3 performances   Attendance, 500

1936

The Merchant of Venice
Twelfth Night
Romeo and Juliet
   Angus Bowmer, Director
5 performances   Attendance, 800

1937

Twelfth Night
The Taming of the Shrew
Romeo and Juliet
   Angus Bowmer, Director
6 performances   Attendance, 1,000

1938

Hamlet
The Taming of the Shrew
Twelfth Night
The Merchant of Venice
   Angus Bowmer, Director
8 performances   Attendance, 2,000

1939

Hamlet
*The Taming of the Shrew**
The Comedy of Errors
As You Like It
   Angus Bowmer, Director
8 performances   Attendance, 2,000

*Also played at the San Francisco
  Exposition

1940

The Merry Wives of Windsor
The Comedy of Errors
As You Like It
Much Ado About Nothing
   William Cottrell, Director
8 performances   Attendance, 1,800

1941 to 1946
Production suspended
during World War II

1947

Hamlet
   Frank Lambrett-Smith, Director
Love's Labour's Lost
   Angus Bowmer, Director
Macbeth
   Angus Bowmer, Director
The Merchant of Venice
   Angus Bowmer, Director
16 performances   Attendance, 4,800

1948

Othello
   Angus Bowmer, Director
The Merchant of Venice
   Angus Bowmer, Director
Love's Labour's Lost
   Angus Bowmer, Director
King John
   Allen Fletcher, Director
16 performances   Attendance, 6,000

1949

Romeo and Juliet
   Richard Graham, Director
Richard II
   James Sandoe, Director
A Midsummer Night's Dream
   James Sandoe, Director
Othello
   Allen Fletcher, Director
The Taming of the Shrew
   Allen Fletcher, Director
20 performances   Attendance, 7,600

1950

Henry IV, Part 1
   Allen Fletcher, Director
As You Like It
   Angus Bowmer, Director
Antony and Cleopatra
   James Sandoe, Director

The Comedy of Errors
   Richard Graham, Director
20 performances   Attendance, 8,850

1951

Twelfth Night
   Richard Graham, Director
Measure for Measure
   James Sandoe, Director
King Lear
   Angus Bowmer, Director
Henry IV, Part 2
   Philip Hanson, Director
24 performances   Attendance, 11,700

1952

The Tempest
   Richard Graham, Director
Julius Caesar
   Allen Fletcher, Director
Henry V
   Philip Hanson, Director
Much Ado About Nothing
   Angus Bowmer, Director
29 performances   Attendance, 15,500

1953

Coriolanus
   Allen Fletcher, Director
The Merchant of Venice
   Richard Graham, Director
Henry VI, Part 1
   James Sandoe, Director
The Taming of the Shrew
   Philip Hanson, Director
29 performances   Attendance, 15,691

1954

Hamlet
   Angus Bowmer, Director
The Winter's Tale
   H. Paul Kliss, Director
The Merry Wives of Windsor
   Allen Fletcher, Director
Henry VI, Part 2
   James Sandoe, Director
31 performances   Attendance, 18,476

1955

A Midsummer Night's Dream
  James Sandoe, Director
Macbeth
  H. Paul Kliss, Director
All's Well That Ends Well
  Robert Loper, Director
Henry VI, Part 3
  James Sandoe, Director
Timon of Athens
  Robert Loper, Director
31 performances   Attendance, 20,243

1956

Richard III
  Allen Fletcher, Director
Love's Labour's Lost
  Allen Fletcher, Director
Romeo and Juliet
  Hal J. Todd, Director
Cymbeline
  B. Iden Payne, Director
Titus Andronicus
  Hal J. Todd, Director
32 performances   Attendance, 19,729

1957

As You Like It
  Angus Bowmer, Director
Othello
  James Sandoe, Director
Two Gentlemen of Verona
  James Sandoe, Director
Henry VIII
  Robert Loper, Director
Pericles, Prince of Tyre
  Robert Loper, Director
31 performances   Attendance, 24,338

1958

Much Ado About Nothing
  Robert Loper, Director
King Lear
  Robert Loper, Director
The Merchant of Venice
  James Sandoe, Director

Troilus and Cressida
  James Sandoe, Director
39 performances   Attendance, 29,652

1959

Twelfth Night
  Angus Bowmer, Director
The Maske of the New World
  by Carl Ritchie
  Jerry Turner, Director
King John
  Richard D. Risso, Director
Measure for Measure
  James Sandoe, Director
Antony and Cleopatra
  James Sandoe, Director
40 performances   Attendance, 36,593

1960

The Taming of the Shrew
  Robert Loper, Director
Julius Caesar
  Jerry Turner, Director
Richard II
  Richard Risso, Director
The Tempest
  James Sandoe, Director
The Duchess of Malfi
  by John Webster
  James Sandoe, Director
41 performances   Attendance, 42,976

1961

All's Well That Ends Well
  Charles Taylor, Director
A Midsummer Night's Dream
  B. Iden Payne, Director
Hamlet
  Robert Loper, Director
Henry IV, Part I
  Richard Risso, Director
The Alchemist
  by Ben Jonson
  Edward Brubaker, Director
42 performances   Attendance, 47,723

1962

As You Like It
  Jerry Turner, Director
The Comedy of Errors
  Rod Alexander, Director
Henry IV, Part II
  Edward Brubaker, Director
Coriolanus
  J. H. Crouch, Director
A Thieves' Ballad
  by Carl Ritchie
  Carl Ritchie, Director
44 performances   Attendance, 44,704

1963

The Merry Wives of Windsor
  Edward Brubaker, Director
Romeo and Juliet
  Robert Loper, Director
Love's Labour's Lost
  Rod Alexander, Director
Henry V
  Jerry Turner, Director
47 performances   Attendance, 51,020

1964

*The Merchant of Venice**
  Rod Alexander, Director
*King Lear**
  Angus Bowmer, Director
*Twelfth Night**
  Robert Loper, Director
Henry VI, Part I
  Jerry Turner, Director
The Knight of the Burning Pestle
  by Francis Beaumont
  Edward Brubaker, Director
58 performances   Attendance, 60,940
*Also played in Frost Amphitheatre,
Stanford, California

1965

Much Ado About Nothing
  James Moll, Director
Macbeth
  Richard Risso, Director

The Winter's Tale
Hugh Evans, Director
Henry VI, Part II
Edward Brubaker, Director
Volpone
by Ben Jonson
Nagle Jackson, Director
48 performances   Attendance, 54,188

1966

ELIZABETHAN STAGE

A Midsummer Night's Dream
Hugh Evans, Director
Othello
Richard Risso, Director
Two Gentlemen of Verona
Nagle Jackson, Director
Henry VI, Part III
Jerry Turner, Director

VARSITY THEATRE

The Beggar's Opera
by John Gay
Carl Ritchie, Director
W. Bernard Windt, Music Director
59 performances   Attendance, 63,092

1967

ELIZABETHAN STAGE

Pericles, Prince of Tyre
Nagle Jackson, Director
Antony and Cleopatra
Jerry Turner, Director
The Taming of the Shrew
Richard Risso, Director
Richard III
Hugh Evans, Director

VARSITY THEATRE

The Maid of the Mill
by Samuel Arnold
Carl Ritchie, Director
W. Bernard Windt, Music Director
63 performances   Attendance, 62,364

1968

ELIZABETHAN STAGE

Cymbeline
James Sandoe, Director
Hamlet
Patrick Hines, Director
As You Like It
William Kinsolving, Director
Henry VIII
Richard Risso, Director

VARSITY THEATRE

Lock Up Your Daughters
from Fielding by Miles, Bart, &
Johnson
Carl Ritchie, Director
W. Bernard Windt, Music Director
63 performances   Attendance, 65,598

1969

ELIZABETHAN STAGE

The Tempest
Richard Risso, Director
Romeo and Juliet
Patrick Hines, Director
Twelfth Night
Hugh Evans, Director
King John
Edward Brubaker, Director

VARSITY THEATRE

Virtue in Danger
from Vanbrugh by Dehn & Bernhard
Carl Ritchie, Director
W. Bernard Windt, Music Director
65 performances   Attendance, 65,710

1970

ANGUS BOWMER THEATRE

You Can't Take It With You
by Moss Hart and George S. Kaufman
Pat Patton, Director
Antigone
by Jean Anouilh
Larry Oliver, Director

The Fantastiks
by Tom Jones and Harvey Schmidt
Peter Nyberg, Director
Larry Carpenter, Music Director
Rosencrantz and Guildenstern are Dead
by Tom Stoppard
Angus Bowmer, Director
The Merchant of Venice
Angus Bowmer, Director
The Imaginary Invalid
by Moliere
Raye Birk, Director

ELIZABETHAN STAGE

The Comedy of Errors
Nagle Jackson, Director
Julius Caesar
Larry Oliver, Director
Richard II
Nagle Jackson, Director
203 performances   Attendance, 126,570

1971

ANGUS BOWMER THEATRE

The Glass Menagerie
by Tennessee Williams
Larry Oliver, Director
A Midsummer Night's Dream
Raye Birk, Director
A Man for All Seasons
by Robert Bolt
Pat Patton, Director
Arsenic and Old Lace
by Joseph Kesselring
Philip Davidson, Director
Under Milk Wood
by Dylan Thomas
Larry Oliver, Director
U. S. A.
by Paul Shyre and John Dos Passos
Jerry Turner, Director

ELIZABETHAN STAGE

Much Ado About Nothing
Larry Oliver, Director
Macbeth
Philip Davidson, Director

Henry IV, Part I
    Pat Patton, Director
233 performances   Attendance, 155,141

1972

ANGUS BOWMER THEATRE

Room Service
    by John Murray and Allen Boretz
    Laird Williamson, Director
The Crucible
    by Arthur Miller
    Pat Patton, Director
Uncle Vanya
    by Anton Chekhov
    Larry Oliver, Director
Playboy of the Western World
    by J. M. Synge
    Jerry Turner, Director
Troilus and Cressida
    Jerry Turner, Director

ELIZABETHAN STAGE

The Taming of the Shrew
    Robert Benedetti, Director
Love's Labour's Lost
    Laird Williamson, Director
Henry IV, Part II
    William Roberts, Director
228 performances   Attendance, 153,335

1973

ANGUS BOWMER THEATRE

Our Town
    by Thornton Wilder
    Pat Patton, Director
The Alchemist
    by Ben Jonson
    Laird Williamson, Director
Othello
    Jerry Turner, Director
The Importance of Being Earnest
    by Oscar Wilde
    James Edmondson, Director
The Dance of Death
    by August Strindberg
    Jerry Turner, Director

ELIZABETHAN STAGE

As You Like It
    Pat Patton, Director
The Merry Wives of Windsor
    Thomas B. Markus, Director
Henry V
    Laird Williamson, Director
224 performances   Attendance, 175,813

1974

ANGUS BOWMER THEATRE

Waiting for Godot
    by Samuel Beckett
    Andrew J. Traister, Director
Hedda Gabler
    by Henrik Ibsen
    Margaret Booker, Director
Two Gentlemen of Verona
    Laird Williamson, Director
The Time of Your Life
    by William Saroyan
    Pat Patton, Director
*A Funny Thing Happened on the Way
to the Forum*
    by Shevelove, Gelbart, and Sondheim
    Jerry Turner, Director
    Todd Barton, Music Director

ELIZABETHAN STAGE

Hamlet
    Jerry Turner, Director
Titus Andronicus
    Laird Williamson, Director
Twelfth Night
    James Edmondson, Director
245 performances   Attendance, 183,187

1975

ANGUS BOWMER THEATRE

The Winter's Tale
    Audrey Stanley, Director
Charley's Aunt
    by Brandon Thomas
    Pat Patton, Director
Oedipus the King
    by Sophocles
    Robert Loper, Director

The Petrified Forest
    by Robert E. Sherwood
    Jerry Turner, Director
Long Day's Journey Into Night
    by Eugene O'Neill
    Jerry Turner, Director

ELIZABETHAN STAGE

Romeo and Juliet
    James Edmondson, Director
All's Well that Ends Well
    Jon Jory, Director
Henry VI, Part I
    Will Huddleston, Director
266 performances   Attendance, 211,518

1976

ANGUS BOWMER THEATRE

The Devil's Disciple
    by Bernard Shaw
    Michael Leibert, Director
The Tavern
    by George M. Cohan
    Pat Patton, Director
Brand
    by Henrik Ibsen
    Jerry Turner, Director
The Comedy of Errors
    Will Huddleston, Director
The Little Foxes
    by Lillian Hellman
    James Moll, Director

ELIZABETHAN STAGE

Henry VI, Part II
    Jerry Turner, Director
Much Ado About Nothing
    James Edmondson, Director
King Lear
    Pat Patton, Director
277 performances   Attendance, 221,317

1977

ANGUS BOWMER THEATRE

Measure for Measure
    Jerry Turner, Director

Angel Street
  by Patrick Hamilton
  Pat Patton, Director
The Rivals
  by R. B. Sheridan
  William Glover, Director
A Streetcar Named Desire
  by Tennessee Williams
  Elizabeth Huddle, Director

ELIZABETHAN STAGE
Henry VI, Part III
  Pat Patton, Director
Antony and Cleopatra
  Robert Loper, Director
The Merchant of Venice
  Michael Addison, Director

BLACK SWAN
A Taste of Honey
  by Shelagh Delaney
  James Edmondson, Director
*A Moon for the Misbegotten**
  by Eugene O'Neill
  Jerry Turner, Director
371 performances   Attendance, 232,368
*Also played at Tao House, Danville,
  California

1978

ANGUS BOWMER THEATRE
Tartuffe
  by Moliere
  Sabin Epstein, Director
Private Lives
  by Noel Coward
  Dennis Bigelow, Director
Mother Courage and Her Children
  by Bertolt Brecht
  Jerry Turner, Director
Timon of Athens
  Jerry Turner, Director
Miss Julie
  by August Strindberg
  Elizabeth Huddle, Director

ELIZABETHAN STAGE
The Taming of the Shrew
  Judd Parkin, Director
Richard III
  Pat Patton, Director
The Tempest
  Michael Addison, Director

BLACK SWAN
The Effect of Gamma Rays on Man-in-the-Moon Marigolds
  by Paul Zindel
  William Glover, Director
Night of the Tribades
  by Per Olov Enquist
  Jerry Turner, Director
434 performances   Attendance, 244,601

1979

ANGUS BOWMER THEATRE
Miss Julie
  by August Strindberg
  Elizabeth Huddle, Director
Macbeth
  Pat Patton, Director
A Midsummer Night's Dream
  Dennis Bigelow, Director
The Play's the Thing
  Ferenc Molnar
  Dennis Bigelow, Director
Born Yesterday
  by Garson Kanin
  James Moll, Director
The Wild Duck
  by Henrik Ibsen
  Jerry Turner, Director

ELIZABETHAN STAGE
As You Like It
  Audrey Stanley, Director
A Midsummer Night's Dream
  Dennis Bigelow, Director
The Tragical History of Dr. Faustus
  by Christopher Marlowe
  Jerry Turner, Director

BLACK SWAN
Who's Happy Now?
  by Oliver Hailey
  Michael Leibert, Director
Root of the Mandrake
  by Niccolo Machieavelli
  Judd Parkin, Director
Indulgences in a Louisville Harem
  by John Orlock
  Michael Kevin, Director
574 performances   Attendance, 265,054

1980

ANGUS BOWMER THEATRE
Coriolanus
  Jerry Turner, Director
Philadelphia Story
  by Philip Barry
  James Moll, Director
As You Like It
  Audrey Stanley, Director
Of Mice and Men
  by John Steinbeck
  Pat Patton, Director
Juno and the Paycock
  by Sean O'Casey
  Michael Kevin, Director
Ring Round the Moon
  by Jean Anouilh
  James Edmondson, Director

ELIZABETHAN STAGE
The Merry Wives of Windsor
  Jon Cranney, Director
Richard II
  Jerry Turner, Director
Love's Labour's Lost
  Dennis Bigelow, Director

BLACK SWAN
Seascape
  by Edward Albee
  Richard Edwards, Director
Sizwe Bansi is Dead
  by Athol Fugard
  Luther James, Director

Lone Star
Laundry and Bourbon
   by James McLure
   Pat Patton, Director
579 performances   Attendance, 264,496

1981

ANGUS BOWMER THEATRE

Wild Oats
   by John O'Keeffe
   Jerry Turner, Director
Twelfth Night
   Pat Patton, Director
Death of a Salesman
   by Arthur Miller
   Robert Loper, Director
'Tis Pity She's a Whore
   by John Ford
   Jerry Turner, Director
Othello
   Sanford Robbins, Director

ELIZABETHAN STAGE

Twelfth Night
   Pat Patton, Director
Two Gentlemen of Verona
   David Ostwald, Director
Henry IV, Part I
   James Edmondson, Director

BLACK SWAN

Artichoke
   by Joanna Glass
   Joy Carlin, Director
The Birthday Party
   by Harold Pinter
   Andrew J. Traister, Director
*The Island**
   by Athol Fugard
   Luther James, Director
571 performances   Attendance, 273,191
*Also toured in California, Washington
  and Oregon

1982

ANGUS BOWMER THEATRE

Blithe Spirit
   by Noel Coward
   Pat Patton, Director
Inherit the Wind
   by Jerome Lawrence and Robert Lee
   Dennis Bigelow, Director
Othello
   Sanford Robbins, Director
Julius Caesar
   Jerry Turner, Director
Spokesong
   by Stuart Parker
   Denis Arndt, Director
The Matchmaker
   by Thornton Wilder
   Rod Alexander, Director

ELIZABETHAN STAGE

*The Comedy of Errors**
   Julian Lopez-Morillas, Director
Romeo and Juliet
   Dennis Bigelow, Director
Henry V
   Pat Patton, Director

BLACK SWAN

Wings
   by Arthur Kopit
   James Moll, Director
Hold Me!
   by Jules Feiffer
   Paul Barnes, Director
The Father
   by August Strindberg
   Jerry Turner, Director
543 performances   Attendance, 288,872
*Also toured Washington and Oregon

1983

ANGUS BOWMER THEATRE

Hamlet
   Robert Benedetti, Director
Man and Superman
   by Bernard Shaw
   James Moll, Director

Ah, Wilderness!
   by Eugene O'Neill
   Jerry Turner, Director
The Matchmaker
   by Thornton Wilder
   Rod Alexander, Director
What the Butler Saw
   by Joe Orton
   Pat Patton, Director
Dracula
   by Richard Sharp
   Richard Geer, Director

ELIZABETHAN STAGE

Much Ado About Nothing
   Dennis Bigelow, Director
Richard III
   Denis Arndt, Director
Cymbeline
   J. H. Crouch, Director

BLACK SWAN

The Entertainer
   by John Osborne
   Dennis Bigelow, Director
*Don Juan in Hell**
   by Bernard Shaw
   James Moll, Director
Dreamhouse
   by Stuart Duckworth
   Jerry Turner, Director
611 performances   Attendance, 302,093
*Also toured in Oregon

1984

ANGUS BOWMER THEATRE

Troilus and Cressida
   Richard E. T. White, Director
London Assurance
   by Dion Boucicault
   Hugh Evans, Director
Dracula
   by Richard Sharp
   Richard Geer, Director
Hay Fever
   by Noel Coward
   James Moll, Director

Cat On a Hot Tin Roof
   by Tennessee Williams
   Pat Patton, Director
The Revenger's Tragedy
   by Cyril Tourneur
   Jerry Turner, Director

ELIZABETHAN STAGE
*The Taming of the Shrew**
   Pat Patton, Director
Henry VIII
   James Edmondson, Director
The Winter's Tale
   Hugh Evans, Director

BLACK SWAN
Translations
   by Brian Friel
   Jerry Turner, Director
Seascape with Sharks and Dancer
   by Don Nigro
   Dennis Bigelow, Director
559 performances   Attendance, 298,560
*Also toured in California

1985

ANGUS BOWMER THEATRE
King Lear
   Jerry Turner, Director
Trelawny of the "Wells"
   by Arthur Wing Pinero
   James Edmondson, Director
Light Up the Sky
   by Moss Hart
   Pat Patton, Director
An Enemy of the People
   by Henrik Ibsen
   Jerry Turner, Director
Crimes of the Heart
   by Beth Henley
   James Moll, Director

ELIZABETHAN STAGE
The Merchant of Venice
   Albert Takazauckas, Director
King John
   Pat Patton, Director

All's Well That Ends Well
   Tony Amendola, Director
BLACK SWAN
Strange Snow
   by Steve Metcalfe
   Andrew J. Traister, Director
The Majestic Kid
   by Mark Medoff
   Edward Hastings, Director
Lizzie Borden in the Late Afternoon
   by Cather MacCallum
   Lou Salerni, Director

The Shakespeare folio in the Margery Bailey Collection, Southern Oregon State College Library.

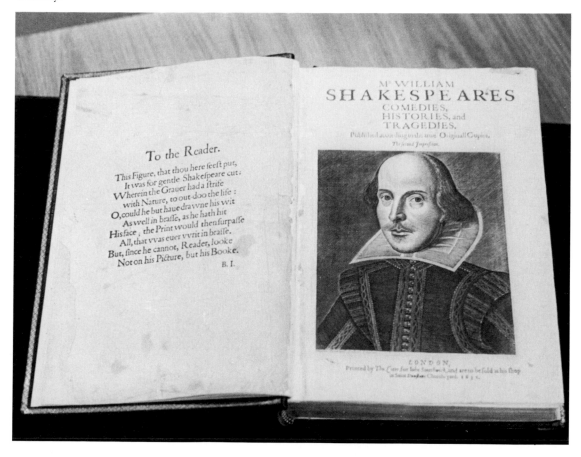

Left: Joan Hotchkis as Lady Gay Spanker
and William McKereghan as Sir Harcourt
Courtly in *London Assurance*, 1984. Costumes
designed by Jeannie Davidson.
Right: Edward Brubaker as Caliban and
Patrick Hines as Prospero in *The Tempest*,
1969. Costumes designed by Jeannie
Davidson.

Carolyn Mason Jones

Design for Ghost in *Hamlet*, 1983, by Jeannie Davidson, Festival costume designer since 1965.

Design for Olivia in *Twelfth Night*, 1964, by
Marie Chesley, Festival costume designer
1961-1964.

PERICLES

THAISA (II-2,3)

SIMONIDES

Byers '67

Design for
Thaisa and Simonides in *Pericles*, 1967,
by Jack A. Byers, Festival costume
designer, 1965-1968.

Design for Theseus in
*A Midsummer Night's
Dream*, 1955, by
Douglas Russell, Festival
costume designer,
1948-1961.

THE FESTIVAL PLAYERS
Compiled by Shirley Patton
The following is an alphabetical list of players who have appeared on Festival stages and the seasons in which they performed. The listing for 1985 is incomplete.

ABBOTT, Bruce Paul 1975–76, 1978
ABBOTT, Christine 1970–71
ABBOTT, Richard 1961
ABERCROMBIE, David M. 1983–84
ABRAMS, Joe 1970
   aka ABRAMCZYCK, Joe
ACKER, Barbara 1968
ADAMS, Deborah 1959–60
ADAMS, William 1983
ADAMSON, John 1980
ADDISON, Michael 1958, 1962
AIKEN, Frances 1935, 1939–40
AINSWORTH, Lynda Lynnea 1971
ALCOCK, Irene 1936
ALDRICH, Wanada 1935
ALDRIDGE, Gary 1964
ALEXANDER, Adrienne 1963, 1975
ALEXANDER, Denise 1963
ALEXANDER, Ray 1956
ALEXANDER, Rod 1961–63
ALEXANDER, Tangren 1955–56
   aka FITCH, Jean
ALLEN, A. Ryan 1969
ALLEN, Kenneth 1954
ALLEN, Lee Anne 1963
ALLEN, Lynessa 1984
ALLEN, Melina 1984
ALLEN, Rex E. 1978–79
ALLIN, Jeffrey 1978
ALPER, Linda 1980–81
ALTO, Robert B. 1970
AMBROSE, Willene 1959
   aka GUNN, Willene
AMENDOLA, Anthony 1978–79
AMES, Jacquelyn 1966
ANDERSEN, Tobias 1983–85
ANDERSEN, Tracy 1978
ANDERSON, Barbara 1949
ANDERSON, Harry 1973
ANDERSON, Stephen 1965
ANDERSON, Suzanne 1966
ANTHONY, Laurence 1961
ARCHAMBAULT, Neville L. 1973–74

A Midsummer Night's Dream, 1979.
Titania asleep in her bower.
Costume design
by Jeannie Davidson.

ARNDT, Denis 1973–77. 1980–83, 1985
ARNOLD, Dick 1984
ARNONE, John 1969–70
ASHBAUGH, Peter O. 1971
ASHWORTH, Jack 1974–75
ASTA, Frank 1966
ASTON, Ruth 1937
ATKINS, Janie E. 1972
AUCLAIR, Len 1971
AVERY, James 1980–82
AYLWARD, John 1983
BACON, Stephen 1980
BAGLEY, Dolores 1950
BAILEY, Margery 1949, 1953
BAIRD, Irene G. 1955–56
BAIRD, Robert E. 1978
BAKER, Beryle 1948
BAKER, Gunther 1984
BAKER, James M. 1952–53, 1955, 1958
BAKER, Jim 1965–66, 1969, 1971
BAKER, Lucian 1962
BALL, William 1951–53
BALLANTYNE, Wayne 1981–85
BALLARD, Everett R. 1983
BALLARD, Laurence 1975–78, 1984
BALLWEG, Dayan 1975
BANISH, Joyce 1936
BARDOSSI, Michael 1981–83
BARKER, John 1935–37
BARNES, Kathleen 1963–64
BARNES, Paul 1982
BARNUM, Les 1968
BARRETT, Patricia 1954
BARRON, Eddy 1947–49
   aka BARRON, Edwin Hugh
BARRY, Paul G. 1951
BARTLETT, Nancy 1961, 1965
BARTON, Todd 1969, 1971, 1976, 1979
BATES, Gerald 1958
BAUGHMAN, Headrick 1939
BAUGHMAN, James 1936–40
BAUGHN, T. Arnold 1937
BAYLESS, Joanne 1967
BEACH, Joe 1939–40
BEACH, Lisa Fortmiller 1963
BEARD, Glorianne 1971
BEARD, Keith 1971
BEARD, Will 1971
BECK, La Murle 1939–40
BECK, Meredith J. 1984
BEDINI, Larry 1959

BEEBE, Barbara 1971
BEECHAM, Jahnna 1977–78
BELL, George H. 1950
BELL, Herbert 1958
BELL, Trubee Joy 1947–48, 1950
    aka WETTERAU, Trubee
BELLAMY, Diana 1970–72
BELLOWS, Gayle 1982–83
BENNETT, Eugene 1940
BENNETT, Michael 1971
BENSON, Robert 1963
BERGEM, Hal 1969
BERGSTROM, Erik B. 1984
BERMAN, Marc 1978
BERNING, Clarissa 1955
BERNINGHAUSEN, Harold 1965–66
BERRY, K. Cecil 1963
BERTRAM, Jean DeSales 1956
BETHENCOURT, John 1952
BIEGLER, Gloria 1982, 1985
BIGLEY, David E. 1953
BILKS, Bess 1949
BILKS, Patrick 1949
BINGHAM, Virginia 1976
BIRK, Candace 1969–71
BIRK, Raye 1969–71, 1974
BISHOP, Randy 1968
BJORLIE, Judy 1964–65, 1970
BLACK, Robert 1966–67
BLAKE-SHEARAN, Ann 1964
BLANKFIELD, Mark 1969–70
BLIEFERNICH, Martin H. 1955
BLUMENFELD, Alan 1975
BOATWRIGHT, Bruce Calvin 1966
BOEN, Earl 1963
BOETTCHER, Karen Sue 1966–68
    aka TATE, Karen
BOKE, Richard Bacon 1955
BONER, Harold 1948
BOOTH, David 1971, 1976
    aka WILLIAMS, David
BOOTH, Eric 1974–75
    aka MILLER, Eric Booth
BOOTHE, Powers 1972–73
BORK, Bob 1974
BOROVKOFF, Francine L. 1978
BOSWELL, Barb 1978
BOUSHEY, Carmi 1975
BOUSHEY, David L. 1975
BOUSSOM, Ron 1970
BOWMAN, Virginia 1957, 1959–60

BOWMER, Angus L. 1935–39,
    1947–54, 1956–59,
    1961–62, 1964, 1966
BOWSER, Randy 1968
BOYD, Howell D. 1955
BRADY, Kathleen 1981
BRAMMER, Clarence 1948–49
BRAND, Robert 1956
BRANDON, Janet 1939
BRANSON, Sue 1950
BREBNER, John 1951
BREIDENTHAL, Tom 1969
BREITLER, Jeff 1984
BRENNAN, Thomas 1952
BRENNEN, Ann 1956
BREULER, Robert 1965
BREWER, Susan 1961–62
BRIDGES, Robert 1962
BRIGANCE, JoAnne 1959
BRODY, Morgan 1951
BROOKS, Jeffrey 1972–75
BROWN, Caryl 1950
BROWN, Franklin 1973–74
BROWN, George 1967
BROWN, Jerry 1970–71
BROWN, Lenore 1953
BROWN, Michael 1965
BRUBAKER, Edward S. 1955–57, 1959–60,
    1962–65, 1969
BUCHANAN, John 1951
BUCHTER, Frank 1947–48
BUFFAM, Dave, Jr. 1971
BUMGARDNER, Don 1958
BUNNELL, Lloyd, Jr. 1948
BUNNELL, Lloyd, Sr. 1948
BURDICK, Hal, Jr. 1950–51
BURGESS, Ralph C., Jr. 1949
BURGIN, J. Raymond 1955
BURK, William 1938
BURKMAN, Marvin C. 1956
BURNS, Robert L. 1979
BURNS, Traber 1980–81
BURROUGHS, Margaret 1939
BURTON, Mouryne 1940
BUTTERFIELD, Catherine 1977
BUTZE, Ed 1935–36
BUTZE, Greta 1936
BYERS, Mollie 1968
CABOT, Christopher 1962
CADIGAN, Michael 1981–82
CAESAR, Adolph 1962

CAIN, Bob 1964
CAJERO, Paul 1964
CALDWELL, George S. 1954
CALDWELL, John A. 1975–76
CALEF, Otis 1965
CALKINS, Kerry 1979
CAMERON, Keith 1971
CAMPBELL, Terry 1956, 1962
CANTWELL, Jack Wellington 1977–79,
    1983–84
CARLON, Pat 1937
CARLSON, Les 1960–62, 1964–65
CARMICHEAL, Lou 1982
    aka CARMICHEAL, Weldon L.
CARNEY, Susan 1984
CARPENTER, Emily 1967–69
CARPENTER, James 1980–83
CARPENTER, Larry 1969–70
CARR, Mimi 1977–80
CARRILLO, Jose 1969
CARRION, Mara 1982
CARSON, Kit 1970
CARSON, Pamela R. 1970
CARTER, Robert 1947–48, 1952
CARTWRIGHT, Jean 1957
CASEY, Timothy 1968
CASSIDY, Dennis L. 1953
CASTEEL, John 1936
CASTELLANOS, John David 1984–85
CAVETT, Dick 1956
CAYWOOD, Paul 1954
CHAMBERLAIN, James 1965
CHANEY, Sally 1971
CHANIK, Jan 1983
CHANIK, John 1983
CHAPMAN, Betti 1964
CHAPMAN, Fred 1963–64
CHAPMAN, Susan 1979
CHASE, Robert 1982–83
CHASE, Scott 1971
CHAVEZ, Edmund M. 1953
CHAVEZ, Joan 1953–54
CHESSE, Dion 1952, 1959
CHESSE, Virginia 1952
CHILDERS, Robert 1940
CHILDS, Casey 1980
CHIPLEY, John 1935
CHRANE, Calvin 1964
CHRISTIANSON, Gary A. 1981–82
CHRISTLIEB, Anthony 1960
CHRISTMAN, Kermit 1972

CHRISTY, Cathy 1967–68, 1970
  aka LINCOLN, Catherine
CHRYSLER, Dave 1939
CHUGG, Gail 1964
CLARK, Carol Jeanne 1968
CLARK, Nancy 1938
CLARK, Rex 1956
CLARK, Vernon 1935
CLAY, Scott 1971
CLEGG, David 1961
CLOVER, John 1978
CLUMPNER, Leslie Ann 1967
COCHRAN, Clinton 1970
COCHRAN, Diane 1954–55, 1957
COCHRAN, Karen 1954–55
COHEN, Robert S. 1962
COHEN, Todd 1983–84
COLDWELL, Charles 1968
COLE, Lois 1954
COLE, Megan 1972–73, 1983
  aka COLE, Elizabeth
COLODNER, Joel 1971–72
COLODNER, Rebecca 1972
COLVIN, Jack 1954–55
COMBS, David 1974
CONDON, Carol 1969
COOK, Carol 1940
COOK, Charles A. 1958
COOK, June 1961
COOK, Morgan 1937
COPE, Betsy 1961, 1963
COPE, Robertson 1961, 1971
COPE, Suzanne 1961
COPPLE, Wilma 1935
CORBETT, Gretchen 1965–66
COREY, Matthew 1963
CORLISS, Guy 1940
COTTON, Michael 1956
COTTRELL, Bill 1935–40
COTTRELL, Nickolas 1954
COURTNEY, Phyllis 1980–83
COVALT, Sara 1963
COWLES, Margaret 1960
COX, Carole 1957
COX, Margaret 1949
COX, Michael 1973
COX, Ruth 1976
COX, Shirley 1960
CRAGGS, Jeffrey 1963
CRAIG, Randall 1967
CRANNEY, Jon 1962–64

CRAWLEY, Patricia 1962
CRENSHAW, Randy 1978
CRENSHAW, Stephen 1973
CRIDER, Lee 1982
CROSS, Claire 1951
CROSSETT, William 1957
CROUCH, Michael 1962
CROUCH, Stephen 1962
CUDDIE, Nanete 1952
CUMMINGS, Beth 1935
CUNNINGHAM, Sean 1964
CURRIER, Patricia 1951
CURTIS, Brad 1951, 1953–56
CURTIS, Lorraine 1954
CURTIS, William 1960
D'ARCY, Timothy 1971–73
D'ARMS, Ted 1955, 1975, 1977
  aka D'ARMS, Edward F.
D'AUTREMONT, Suzanne 1963
DANFORD, Doris 1939–40
DANIELS, Clara 1948–53
  aka REINHARDT, Clara Daniels
DANIELS, James 1975
DARLING, Joan 1955–56
  aka KUGELL, Joan
DARNEILLE, Don 1935, 1948
DARRAH, John R. 1970
DAUGHERTY, Byron DeWitt 1966
DAUGHERTY, Jeanne 1935
DAVENPORT, Evelyn C. 1967
DAVENPORT, Patricia 1964
DAVID, Agnes 1955
DAVIDSON, Evan 1973, 1979–80, 1982
DAVIDSON, Hilary 1980, 1984
DAVIDSON, Lawrence E. 1963–65
DAVIDSON, Philip 1967–73, 1979–85
DAVIES, Helen 1953–54
  aka PEPPARD, Helen Davies
DAVIES, John 1961
DAVIS, Ada 1940
DAVIS, Carol 1966
DAVIS, Danny 1968
DAVIS, Diantha 1964
DAVIS, Gordon 1938
DAVIS, Jason 1984
DAVIS, Josephine 1947
DAVIS, Lillian 1939
DAVIS, Luciano 1939
DAVIS, Rueben 1983
DAVIS, Susan E. 1983
DAVIS, William H. 1947

DAWKINS, Christopher 1963–65
DAWKINS, Ellen 1961, 1963
DAWKINS, Michael 1953, 1955
DAY, Melba 1938
  aka SPARKS, Melba Day
DAY, Michael 1976
DAY, Nancy 1938
DE BERRY, David C. 1972
DE GUSTA, Ken 1967
DE LAUBENFELS, Diane 1962
DE LISLE, Betty 1940
DE LLAMAS, Kathleen 1984
DE SALVIO, Joseph 1972–77, 1981, 1983–85
  aka VINCENT, Joe
DE SALVIO, Melody 1984
DE SANTIS, Patrick 1977–79
DEAN, Anne 1940
DEFILIPPIS, Leonardo 1979–80
DEL GRANDE, Louis 1965
DENISON, Richard 1977–78, 1983–84 '
DESMOND, Dan 1973
DEVER, Joyce 1968
DEXTER, Corky 1984–85
DIMEO, Diane 1972
DOBBS, John 1960
DODSON, Barbara 1948
DOKEY, Cameron 1977–80
DOLAS, Lura 1984
DOMINGUEZ, Juan A. 1984
DONADIO, James A. 1974
DONALDSON, Tom 1966–67, 1969–72
DONOHUE, Michael 1971
DORFMAN, Ronald 1963
DORRIS, George 1949
DORSEY, Sherman 1967
DOUGLAS, Randi 1965, 1975
DOUGLASS, Shirley 1958–65, 1967–83, 1985
  aka PATTON, Shirley
DOWIS, Pamala 1963
DOWNEY, Leo 1984
DREWES, Stephen R. 1971
DU RAND, le Clanche 1973–75
DUBOIS, Louise 1938
DUCKWORTH, Stuart 1978–83
DUKE, Paul 1980–81
DUNCAN, Michael 1985
DUNHAM, Clyde 1940
DUNHAM, Jim 1984
DUNN, Dwight 1968
DUNN, Maryann K. 1971
DUPUIS, Adele 1948

DURHAM, Weldon 1966
DURNELL, Tom 1972
DWYER, Mavourneen 1971
DYNARSKI, Eugene 1962
EAGAN, Michael 1973
EAKLE, David 1977, 1979
EBERHART, Bill 1935
EBERT, Michael 1954
EBEY, George 1963–64
ECKSTEIN, Ann 1950–51
    aka GUILBERT, Ann
ECKSTEIN, George 1948, 1950, 1952
EDELMAN, Charles 1968–69
EDMISTON, Helen 1935
EDMONDSON, James 1972–77,
    1979–81, 1984–85
EDSTROM, Nicole 1975
EDWARDS, Richard Allan 1970–72
EISENBERG, Muriel 1957
EITZE, Chester 1965
ELBERSON, Stanley 1963
ELLENBERGER, Helen 1935–36
ELLER, Carol 1949–50
ELLIOTT, Malinke 1980
ELLIOTT, Mary F. 1966
ELLIOTT, Russell 1968
ELLISON, Carol 1950
ELMGREN, Charlotte 1963
ELMORE, Richard 1980–85
ERNST, Carol 1979–82
ERWIN, William 1951–52
ESPESETH, Miriam 1972
ESSARY, Don 1960
ESTERBROOK, Richard 1983–84
EUSTICE, George 1978
EVANS, Derek 1968
EVANS, Hugh C. 1958, 1960–64
EVANS, Kenneth 1940
EVANS, Mary G. 1957
EVANS, William 1973
FADDEN, Walt 1982
FAIRCHILD, Tom 1938–39
FAIRWEATHER, Chloe 1951
FAIRWEATHER, Don 1952
FARMER, Richard 1940
FARRELL, Patricia 1939
FARRELL, Richard 1977–78
FEARON, Allen 1969
FEDERICO, Donna 1969
FELDMAN, Joseph 1975
FERRER, Leticia 1961

FERRITER, William 1976, 1978
FIELDS, James 1983
FIELDS, Robert 1954
FILLMORE, Kent 1972
FINNEGAN, James 1981–82
FISCHER, Stefan 1982
FISH, Peter 1954
FITCH, Jean 1955–56
    aka ALEXANDER, Tangren
FLETCHER, Allen 1948–50, 1952–54, 1956
FLETCHER, Diana 1961
FLICK, Virginia 1963
FOLIE, Michael T. 1979–80
FORSYTH, Grace 1938
FOSTER, Jim 1935–36
FOUCH, Elizabeth 1940
FOWLER, Keith 1958, 1960
FOWLER, Knox 1953–54
FOWLER, Suzanne 1953–54
FRANK, Eileen 1955
FRASER, Buzz 1983–84
FRAZIER, Robert 1947
FREEMAN, Tom 1983
FRENCH, Dorothy 1969–70
FRIEDLANDER, Larry 1981
FRISBIE, Carol 1948
FRISHMAN, Danny 1978–79
FROEHLICH, Peter 1965
FROHNMAYER, Mira 1959
FROST, Marion 1935–36
    aka FROST, Jack
FRYER, Lockhart 1972
FUCHS, Michael 1960–62
    aka FUCHS, Milton
FULLER, Glenn 1940
FULTON, Philip 1952
FULTZ, Mona Lee 1974
GAGE, Robert 1971
GALLAGHER, Lynne 1958
GAMBLE, William 1963
GANTNER, Carrillo 1968
GARCIA, David V. 1954
GARDNER, Craig 1970
GARDNER, Craig R. 1979
GARDNER, Gerald 1952–53
GATCHELL, Jerry 1966
GAVIGAN, John M. 1968
GAVIN, Greg 1977
GEARHART, Errilla 1936
GEARY, Sallie 1938
GEISSLINGER, Bill 1980–81, 1985

GEIST, Kenneth 1957
GETGOOD, John 1963–64
GETGOOD, Mary 1964
GIANCARLO, Jim 1977, 1981–82
GIBSON, Kirk 1974
GIFFIN, Peter 1979–80
GILL, Susan 1965
GILLESPIE, Carolyn 1973
GILLIS, Alex 1973
GILROY, Nicholas 1949–50
GLASSBERG, Lynn 1950
GLENN, James 1940
GLENN, Timothy 1983–84
GODSEY, Lynette 1973
GODWIN, Stephen J. 1979–80
GOFF, Jo 1971–73
GOFF, Tina Marie 1982
GOOCH, Bruce T. 1978–83
GOODHUE, John Scott 1965
GORDON, Lindy 1956
GORDON, William 1984
GORMAN, Jo Firestone 1965
GOTTFRIED, Dolores 1953
GOULD, Harold 1958
GOURLEY, George 1978
GRADY, Matthew 1978
GRAHAM, Bruce 1951–52
GRAHAM, Jennifer 1969
GRAHAM, Mari 1975
GRAHAM, Martha Ann 1963–64
GRAHAM, Richard 1948–58, 1963–64
GRANT, Keith 1976–78
GRANT, Wesley 1983, 1985
GRAY, Eldridge 1940
GREEN, Kenneth 1950
GREER, Herb 1950–51
GREER, Skip 1984–85
GREGORY, William 1958–59
GROSSMAN, Alice 1938–39
GROSSMAN, Alice 1962
GROUND, Robert 1968–69
GROVE, Gregory 1970
GROVER, Edward 1958–59
GROVER, Mark 1976
GRUNDLACH, Daniel 1972
GUENTHER, Benard Paul 1971
GUILBERT, Ann 1950–51
    aka ECKSTEIN, Ann
GUILEY, Max 1936
GUILEY, Peggy 1936
GUNDERSON, Don 1950, 1956

GUNN, Willene 1959
   aka AMBROSE, Willene
GUNTER, Merrill 1935
GURAL, Ron 1968
GUTHRIE, Jo Bailey 1968–69
HAAG, Richard 1950
HACKNEY, Ann 1960, 1967–68
   aka KINSOLVING, Ann
HADLEY, Douglas 1973–74
HAILEY, Marian 1962–63
HAINES, Eleanor Alice 1949
HALES, John 1961
HALES, Mary Jane 1961
HALL, Arden 1937–38, 1940, 1947
HALL, Michael Keys 1974–75
HALL, Sands 1976
HAMILTON, Betsy Sacks 1966–68
   aka SACKS, Betsy Lee
HAMILTON, Norman 1937–38
HAMILTON, Rick 1966–68, 1970–71,
   1978–79
HAMMER, Mark 1959–60
HANLEY, Jeff 1972
HANSEN, Warren 1976
HANSON, Curtis 1969
HANSON, Luther 1982
HANSON, Philip 1949–53, 1959
HANSON, Suzanne LaMarre 1947–53
   aka LA MARRE, Suzanne
HANSON, Torrey 1984–85
HARBOUR, James 1973
HARDY, Frances E. 1937
HARDY, Jonathan 1967
HARELIK, Mark 1976
HARING, Lee 1956
HARPER, Paul 1958, 1960
HARR, John 1935
HARRER, David 1982
HARRIS, Joyce 1981–82
HARRIS, Mary Elizabeth 1961
HARRISON, Jon 1968
HARRISON, Mark 1974
HART, David A. 1970–71, 1975
HART, Mary 1977
HASTINGS, Hugh 1983–84
HATTAN, Mark 1948
HAUSOTTER, Jack O. 1949
HAWKINS, John 1959
HAY, Richard L. 1950, 1956, 1964
HAYNES, Larry 1967–69
HAYS, Dan 1964–68

HAYS, Terry 1977–78
HEALY, Christine 1974–77
HEATH, Annabel 1937
HEFLIN, Gabriel 1983
HEGDAHL, Dave 1974
HEITZ, Lyle 1937
HEJNA, Jim 1978
HELDE, Annette 1980–81
HELLMUTH, Georg W. 1952
HENRY, Shane 1983
HENSELMAN, Phil 1940
HERNDON, David 1949
HERNDON, Laurel 1949
HERNON, Bill 1947
HERRING, Jennifer 1967
HERRITT, Keith 1975
HERZOG, John 1969
HESS, Penelope 1964
HIBBARD, Donald 1948–49
HIGGINS, Dennis 1968
HIGH, Bradley 1970
HILL, Hollis 1947–48
HILL, James Barton 1971–72
HILL, Michael J. 1975
HILLER, Elizabeth 1958
HILLGARTNER, Malcolm 1978–79
HILLIARD, Robert J. 1951
HILLSBURY, Jack 1939
HINES, Patrick 1952–53, 1968–69
   aka HINES, Mainer
HIRSCHBOECK, Robert 1979–81
HIRTZEL, Lawrence 1968
HITCHCOCK, George 1957
HODGKINSON, Anne 1981
HOGAN, Michael R. 1977
HOGUE, Ross 1951
HOKIN, Harlin 1973–74
HOLLAND, Glenn 1973
HOLLAND, Jon 1968–69
HOLLOWAY, Jerry 1956
HONEYWELL, Scott 1984
HOOPER, Susan 1965
HOOSER, Dick 1967
HOPPE, Daniel J. 1962–63
HOPPE, Judith 1963
HORN, Bob 1967
HORTON, Michael 1975
HORTON, Steven 1969
HOTCHKIS, Joan 1984
HOTELL, Maybelle 1940
HOULE, Ray 1977–78

HOWARD, Christopher 1969
HOWARD, Dana 1969
HOWARD, Ezra 1959
HOWARD, Mary Jane 1947
HOWELL, Ghent 1969
HOYT, Judson L. 1983
HUBBARD, Brenda 1983–84
HUBBARD, Douglas Gar 1940
HUBBARD, Robin 1969
HUBERT, Lawrence 1936
HUDDLE, Elizabeth 1961–64, 1977
HUDDLESTON, Will 1971–76
HUDSON, David 1977
HUFMAN, Don 1940
HUGGINS, Barbara 1951, 1959
   aka WAIDE, Barbara
HUGHES, Allan 1963
HULL, Ilene 1947
HULL, Margaret 1956
HULME, Mike 1965
HUME, John 1948
HUME, Kathryn 1948
HUMMASTI, Arnold 1967–68, 1973
HUMPHREY, A. Bryan 1974
HUNNELL, Maxine Gearhart 1935–37
HUNT, Constance 1948
HUNT, Elise 1961
HUNTER, Alana 1977–78
HURT, William 1975
HUSTON, J. Wesley 1980–81
HUTCHINS, Frank 1947
HUTCHINS, Grant 1947
INGLE, Kitty 1936–38
ISSER, Jacob 1984
JACKSON, Al Stuart 1953
JACKSON, Cricket 1983
JACKSON, Nagle 1957–59, 1961, 1965–67
JACOBS, James David 1982
JACOBUS, Philip 1956
JAMES, Katherine 1975
JANES, Dolph 1935
JENKINS, Claude 1953, 1958
   aka WOOLMAN, Claude
JENNINGS, Byron 1971–72
JENNINGS, Nancy 1957
JENNY, Paul 1977, 1983
JESSUP, Richard 1979, 1981
JOHNSON, Andrew 1935
JOHNSON, Dan 1971, 1973
JOHNSON, Daryl 1971
JOHNSON, David 1970

JOHNSON, Gregg 1983–84
JOHNSON, JoAnn 1975–79, 1982, 1984
  aka PATTON, JoAnn Johnson
JOHNSON, Johnie 1949
JOHNSON, Linda 1965–66, 1968
JOHNSON, Richard 1947
JOLLY, Joyce 1966
JONES, Beverly 1940
JONES, Bob 1981
JONES, Christopher 1958
JONES, David H. 1964, 1966
JONES, Jerry 1976–77
JONES, Jill 1983
JONES, Laura 1940
JONES, Marilyn 1976
JONES, Philip L. 1975–76
JONES, Richard T. 1955
JOYCE, Nancy 1970–71
JUDD, Terry 1969
KAHLO, James Grant 1953, 1956
KALISH, Abe 1955
KALLOK, Andy 1970
KALLUS, Bob 1976
KAMITSES, Zoe 1965–66
KAMMEN, Shira 1981–82
KANNASTO, Sherril 1972–73, 1981–83
KASDAN, Michael F. 1955–56
KAST, Carolynne 1984
KAY, Ellen 1957–58
KAYE, Naomi 1949
KEACH, Stacy 1962–63
KEATING, Marianne 1949
KEATING, Timothy 1949
KEELER, William 1982–84
KEENEY, Darrell 1953
KEITH, Brian Edward 1972
KELLER, Elisabeth 1964
KELLY, Frank 1968, 1970
KELLY, Noreen 1947–48
KEMP, Brandis 1970
  aka KEMP, Vivian Sally
KEMP, Jules 1960
KENNEDY, Judith 1955–56, 1958–63, 1983
  aka OFFORD, Judith
KENT, Enid 1965–66
KERN, Dan 1971
KESSLER, Scott 1984
KEVIN, Michael 1971–75, 1978–79, 1982–83
  aka MOORE, Garry
KILMURRY, Maureen 1979–80
KING, Katherine 1970

KING, Ninon 1940, 1947
KING, Ruth Elodie 1978
KINNEY, Harry 1971
  aka KINNEY, Alex
KINSOLVING, Ann 1960, 1967–68
  aka HACKNEY, Ann
KINSOLVING, William 1960–61
KLISS, H. Paul 1951–55
KNECHT, Alexander 1980, 1982
KNIES, Richard 1962
KNOWLES, Arlieta 1957
KNOX, Margaret 1936–37
KOEHLER, John S. 1968
KOON, Theresa 1979
KOS, Ann 1938–39
KOZOL, Roger 1969–70
KRAFT, Barry 1980–85
KRAMER, Wayne 1964
KRAUS, Philip 1971
KRAUSE, Gisela 1971
KREK, Lydia Tatjana 1983
KREMER, Dan 1976–79, 1985
KRILL, Anne 1981
KRUG, Teresa 1967
KRUGEL, Loisgae 1940
KRUSER, Jim 1971
KUBALEK, Sandra 1959
KUGELL, Joan 1955–56
  aka DARLING, Joan
KURR, Mary Alice 1974
KYLE, Jean Arden 1954
LA MARRE, Suzanne 1947–53
  aka HANSON, Suzanne La Marre
LACY, Brian 1975
LAGOMARSINO, Ron 1972
LAMB, Ralph 1939
LAMBERT, Mark E. 1983
LAMBRETT-SMITH, Frank 1947
LANCHESTER, Duane 1954
LANDRO, Vincent 1966–68
LANE, Addyse 1950–51
LANE, David 1966
LANGENSTEIN, Perry 1966
LARIVE, Ann Marie 1966
LARSEN, William 1953
LARSON, Gerard 1960–61
LAUGHLIN, Stuart 1948
LAURIS, Anna 1983
LAURIS, Priscilla Hake 1982–83, 1985
LAUTERER, Alice 1956
LAWDER, Anne 1950

LAWSON, Robert 1966
LAWSON, Ted 1960
LEAHY, Michael 1977
LEARMAN, Richard 1953
LEBERER, Michael 1974
LEE, Dorothy 1940
LEE, Jason 1973
LEE, Wayne 1975
LEGGETT, Manley 1940
LEGGETTE, Christopher 1970
LEIBERT, Michael 1961
LEONARD, Aldena 1973
LEONARD, Jean 1951
LEONARD, Richard 1972–73
LEROY, Zoaunne 1983
LEVER, Robert C. 1947
LEVERETTE, Doreen 1936–38
LEVERING, Linda 1962–63
LEVITOW, Roberta 1976
LEWIS, April 1963–65
LEWIS, Arthur 1959
LEWIS, Barbara 1950
LEWIS, Bonda 1965
LEWIS, Caroline 1961
LEWIS, Cooper A. 1978–80
LEWIS, Courtney 1979–80
LEWIS, E. Bonnie 1975
LEWIS, Owen B. 1983
LEWIS, Ray 1939
LIMA, Toni 1983–84
LINCOLN, Catherine 1967–68, 1970
  aka CHRISTY, Cathy
LINCOLN, Richard 1966–67, 1970
LINDBLOM, Ron 1980
LINDNER, Leroy 1937–40
LIVINGSTON, Bert 1948
LIVINGSTON, William 1960
LLOWELL, Odysseus 1974
LO VINE, David 1980–84
LOCKE, Bob 1965
LOCKE, Vivian Stevenson 1949
LOFTSGAARD, Benny 1947
LOGAN, Sandy 1967
LOMBARDO, Philip 1979
LONGAN, Jay 1974
LOOMIS, Kevin 1981
LOPER, Robert B. 1955, 1958, 1960
LOPER, Shirley M. 1957
LOPEZ-MORILLAS, Julian 1970–72
LORING, Edna 1947, 1949
LORR, Tamara K. 1983–84

LOTT, Lawrence C. 1979
LOUGHRIDGE, Gregg 1983–84
LOVBERG, Marjorie 1952
LOVE, Jeanne 1950
LOWE, Malcolm 1984
LOWRY, Nina M. 1966
LOWRY, Robert 1972
LUCE, Thomas 1955
LUEBBE, Alda 1938
LUNGREEN, Margo 1948
LURIA, Idalah 1969
LYMAN, Kenneth 1965
LYNCH, Kevin 1983
LYNCH, Sandy 1973–74
LYNNER, Brian 1976
MAASKE, Dee 1984–85
MAC DOUGALL, Robert 1978
MAC IVER, Kenned 1977–78
MAC KENZIE, Will 1960
MAC LACHLAN, Kyle 1982
MACARTHUR, Alicia Ruhl 1938
MACHIN-SMITH, Helen 1982–83
MACKEY, Martin 1976
MACLEAN, Dorothy 1961
MACLEAN, Peter D. 1961–62
MACPHEE, John T. 1955
MACWHIRTER, Don 1950
MADDOX, Raoul 1974
MADDOX, Todd 1978
MADISON, James 1954
MAGRUDER, Michael 1977
MAILLARD, Josephine 1955
MAJOR, Kathryn G. 1984
MANLOVE, John 1949–50
MANN, Craig 1968
MANSFIELD, John 1974
MARAVIGLIA, Larry 1965
MARCUSE, Theodore 1959
MARKHAM, Monte 1961
MARKKANEN, Douglas 1983–85
MARKUS, Tom 1957
MARRS, Bruce 1982
MARSHALL, Linda 1961
MARSHALL, Ted 1940
MARSTON, David 1975–77, 1979–80, 1982
MARSTON, Sue 1976–77, 1979, 1983
MARTIN, Adrian E. 1939
MARTIN, Elva 1936
MARTIN, Kathryn 1972
MARTIN, Larry 1966, 1971
MARTIN, Phillip 1983

MARTIN, Steven 1983–85
MARTIN, Thomas 1967–68
MASON, Dean 1949
MASON, Marylee 1953
MASTERSON, Michael 1984
MATTHEWS, Gordon 1951
MAYES, Daniel 1981–83
MAZEN, Glenn 1967
MC ANINCH, Elizabeth 1972
MC ARTHUR, Jane 1949–50
MC BROOM, Amanda 1968–69
MC CARLEY, Isaac 1949–52
MC CARRELL, Michael 1984–85
MC CLAREN, Bill 1968
MC CORMICK, Hank 1967
MC CORNACK, Bryn Alison 1971
MC COY, Patty 1970, 1974
MC COY, William 1971
MC CRACKEN, Sharon 1947
MC DONOUGH, Ruth 1949
MC DOUGALL, Jerry 1947, 1949
MC DOUGALL, Leon 1949
MC GANTY, Ken 1971–72
MC KAY, Donald 1949
MC KAY, Rhys 1966
MC KEREGHAN, William 1983–85
MC KINLEY, Mary Lou 1959
MC KINNIS, Ralph 1947
MC KOVICH, Maureen 1966
MC LAIN, Sidney 1966–67
MC LELLAN, Herbert 1958
MC LEOD, Bruce 1970
MC LURE, James 1970
MC MAHON, Terri 1984
MC NAIR, Marjorie 1936
MC NAMARA, Patrick 1968
MC PHEE, Norman 1957
MEDALIS, Joseph G. 1967
MEE, Kirk 1962–65
MEEKER, Douglas 1952
MEEKER, Ellie 1955
MEINKE, Garold 1953
MELINAT, Lucille 1963–64
MERIN, Eda Reiss 1954
MERRIFIELD, Randall 1972
MERRIMAN, Esther Carter 1937–38
METROPOLIS, Penny 1985
METSKAS, Judith 1974
METZGER, Lulu 1938
MICHAEL, Eileen 1948
MICKEY, Jerry 1957

MIKELSON, Ivars 1982–84
MILLER, Charles 1961–62
MILLER, Eric Booth 1974–75
    aka BOOTH, Eric
MILLER, Howard 1953
MILLS, Terry 1972
MIMS, Mary Ellen 1949
MINTER, Wanda 1937
MITCHELL, Dolores Y. 1976
MOE, Margit 1973–74
MOFFAT, Mary Jane 1949–50
    aka PITTS, Mary Jane
MOLLOY, William 1970
MOLODOVSKY, Mary 1978
MONAHAN, Laurie 1972–74
MONICH, Tim 1972
MONROE, Duain 1939
MONROE, Jarion 1983
MOORE, Angus 1938
MOORE, Daniel 1976–77, 1979
MOORE, Garry 1971–75, 1978–79, 1982–83
    aka KEVIN, Michael
MOORE, Hagan 1938
MOORE, John 1948
MOORE, Karl 1935–36
MOORE, Randall 1969
MORAN, Patricia 1958
MOREING, William 1975–77
MORIN, Rosa 1969
MORELY, James 1952
MORTON, Hugh 1957
MOSCRIP, Carol 1959
MOSES, Emily 1973
MOSES, Harry 1940
MULHOLLAND, Barry 1975–77
MULHOLLAND, Brian 1976–77
MURPHEY, Mark 1969–70, 1973–75, 1982–84
MURPHY, Ric 1961–62
MURPHY, Russell A. 1966
MYERS, Lou 1979
MYRVOLD, Paul 1972–73
MYRVOLD, Sylvia 1973
NAHOE, Pancho 1971
NALE, David Kent 1967–78
NAUSE, Allen 1975–77, 1983–84
NELSON, Arnold 1952
NELSON, Frederick B. 1949
NELSON, Saundra 1972
NESS, Eric 1981
NEUMAN, Gayle Stuwe 1975–77
NEUMAN, Phil 1974, 1976–77

NEWCOMB, Steve 1975
NEWELL, Michael 1981
NEWMAN, Rick 1970
NEWPORT, Rosalyn 1956–58
NEWTON, Christopher 1960–61
NIBLEY, Alexander 1977
NICKERSON, Chet 1975
NININGER, Logan 1936
NOLAND, Charles 1983
NORAAS, Knut Jarl 1982
NORDWICH, Harry A. 1947
NORELL, Michael 1964
NORMAN, Patricia 1950
NORRIS, Karen 1982
NORTON, Carolyn 1969
NORWALK, John 1979–80
NOURSE, Kathleen 1937
NOURSE, Roberta 1937
NYBERG, Peter 1970
NYE, William 1958–60
O'BRIEN, David 1956–57, 1959
O'CONNOR, Paul Vincent 1982–85
O'NEIL, Bradford 1975, 1982
O'SCANNELL, Patricia Maureen 1981–82, 1984
O'SULLIVAN, Michael 1957–58, 1970
OFFORD, Judith 1955–56, 1958–63, 1983
   aka KENNEDY, Judith
OHANNESIAN, David 1972
OLENIACZ, Tom 1967–69, 1977–78
OLESON, Todd 1974–75
OLIVER, Larry 1970
OLSON, Brigit 1978–79
OLSON, Eric 1978–79
OLSTER, Fredi 1970–71, 1978–79
OMEIRS, Patrick 1967
ONOFRIO, Michael 1952
ONSTAD, Mike 1965
ONTIVEROS, William P. 1977
OPDENAKER, Susan 1974
OREM, David 1966
OSTRANDER, Arthur 1947
OSTRANDER, Paula 1947
OSTWALD, David 1962
OWEN, David 1967
OWEN, Wesley 1958
OYLER, William 1951–52, 1954–57, 1959, 1966
PADGETT, George 1949
PAGE, Melody Ann 1977–78
PAGE, Robert 1964–65
PAGE, Robert, Jr. 1964–65
PAGLIUCA, Sally 1962

PAKE, Greg 1983
PALMER, Robert 1961
PALMER, Tom 1935
PAOLETTI, Lynne 1956
PAPPAS, Victor 1974
PARKER, James 1956
PARKIN, Judd 1975–77
PARKINSON, Sue 1940
PARKS, Ellyn Sue 1960
PARRENT, Leon 1949–50
PARSONS, Jim 1937–38
PATNAUDE, Greg 1983
PATTERSON, Donald 1965
PATTERSON, Steven 1981–82
PATTON, JoAnn Johnson 1975–79, 1982, 1984
   aka JOHNSON, JoAnn
PATTON, Kent 1971
PATTON, Kimberly 1980, 1982–84
PATTON, Kristin Anne 1972–73, 1975–78, 1981–82
PATTON, Pat 1964–66, 1970–73, 1975, 1978–79
PATTON, Pat, III 1978, 1980, 1982–83
PATTON, Shirley 1958–65, 1967–83, 1985
   aka DOUGLASS, Shirley
PATTON, Will 1975, 1977
PATTON, William W. 1949–51
PAULSEN, Jeanne 1980–83, 1985
PAULSEN, Lawrence 1980–83, 1985
PAVLISIN, Steve 1956
PAYNE, B. Iden 1956
PEARCE, Paulina 1958
PEARL, Matt 1972
PEDRICK, Marcia 1974
PEJOVICH, Theodore 1969
PENDER, Jay 1950
PEOTTER, Pauline 1956–58
PEPPARD, George 1951, 1953–54
PEPPARD, Helen Davies 1954
   aka DAVIES, Helen
PERCIVAL, Michael 1962
PEREZ, Kenneth 1970
PERKINS, Bob 1939
PERKOVICH, David 1969
PERRY, Gene 1939
PETERS, Mary Ed 1967, 1969
   aka PORTER, Mary Ed
PETERSEN, Anne 1962
PEYROUX, Eugene 1961
PFEIFFER, P. L. 1955
PHELPS, Corey 1970

PHELPS, Emily 1971–72
PHELPS, Jolene 1970
   aka VAN HOOSER, Jolene
PHELPS, Sabine 1959
PHILLIPS, Maureen Thompson 1981
PHIPPS, Gerald 1970
PICKHARDT, Nancy 1956
PIERCE, Michael 1960
PINNOCK, Betty 1953
PINNOCK, Frank S. 1953–55
PIPER, Roland 1947–48, 1954
PITTS, Mary Jane 1949–50
   aka MOFFAT, Mary Jane
PLIKAITIS, Theresa 1984
PLOCHER, Deborah 1956
PLUCINSKI, Dan 1969
POE, Hal 1967
POE, Michael 1967
POE, Richard 1981–82
PONCH, Martin 1953
POND, Ray Keith 1965–66
POND, Sam 1981–82
PONDER, Samuel 1981
PONTON, Richard 1966
POPPE, Herman 1964–65
PORTER, Mary Ed 1967, 1969
   aka PETERS, Mary Ed
PORTER, Scott 1967–69
POTOZKIN, Amy 1983
PRATT, Emerson 1936
PRELLE-TWOREK, Martin 1984
PRENDERGAST, Monica 1971
PRICE, Marsha 1966
PRIESTLY, Harry 1938
PRITCHETT, Daniel 1978–79
PROBST, Nicholas 1953
PROCACCINO, John 1977
PROSSER, Eleanor 1952–54
PRUITT, Dorothy 1935–39
PRUITT, Lyman S. 1956–58
PUCKETT, Richard 1951
QUINBY, James 1983
QUINBY, Priscilla 1984
QUINBY, William A. 1983
QUINN, Deborah 1969
RABOLD, Rex 1976–80
RAMOS, S. Richard 1962
RAMSDELL, Marilyn 1940
RAMSEY, Diane 1975
RAMSEY, Jeffrey 1977
RAMSEY, Mack 1974–79

RAMSEY, Sarah Mead 1978–79
RANDALL, Juliet 1957, 1959
    aka RANDALL, Mary Jo
RANTAPAA, Ray A. 1971
RAWE, Mary Pat 1939–40
RAWSON, Mark 1959
REED, Betty Sue 1940
REED, Franklin 1948
REEDER, Andrea 1963
REEDY, Harold 1937
REICHENBACH, Todd 1975
REID, Robert M. 1979–80
REID, Sarah 1984
REINES, Philip 1958
REINHARDT, Clara Daniels 1948–53
    aka DANIELS, Clara
REINHARDT, Paul 1951–52
REISACHER, John 1937–40
REISS, Belinda 1963
RENFORTH, John 1974
RENNER, Daniel 1984–85
REYNOLDS, Edgar 1958
REYNOLDS, Richard 1974
RHOADS, Betty 1940
RHOADS, Gene 1940
RICHARDSON, Douglas 1965
RICHARDT, Dave 1972
RICHMOND, Charles 1963
RIDDLE, George 1957–58
RIEHLE, Richard 1972–74, 1980–81
RIGGS, Joel 1959
RILEY, Molly 1961, 1967
    aka RISSO, Molly
RILEY, Richard 1977
RILEY, Susan 1978–79
RINGER, James 1974
RISSO, Molly 1961, 1967
    aka RILEY, Molly
RISSO, Richard 1952–54, 1959–61, 1965,
    1967, 1969
RISTOFF, Anthony 1958–59
RITCHIE, Bill 1983
RITCHIE, Carl 1950, 1957, 1959–61
ROBBINS, Rebecca 1975
ROBERTS, Diane 1972
ROBERTS, Maryen 1948–49
ROBERTS, William 1963–65, 1967, 1972
ROBINSON, Bob 1966
RODGER, David 1971
RODGERS, J. Gerald 1962
ROGERS, Forbes "Buck" 1969–70

ROGERS, Julie 1970
ROGERS, Rodney 1936–37
ROISUM, Ted 1982
ROLAND, Paul 1985
ROLL, Schuyler 1970
ROMANO, Ethel Mae Robinett 1940
ROME, Jon 1976
ROOKLYN, Dale Thomas 1977
ROOT, Bob 1935–36
RORVIK, Alice 1972
ROSS, Fred I. 1947
ROSS, Richard 1976
ROSSI, Richard 1977–79
ROTH, Kenneth W. 1970–71
ROTH, Norman 1964
ROVERE, Craig 1982–83
ROYSTON, William 1962
RUBIN, Margaret 1957–59, 1975, 1977–80,
    1982–83, 1985
    aka VAFIADIS, Margaret
RUCKER, Judi 1966
RUCKER, Pat 1966
RUDOLPH, P. A. 1968
RUPPECK, John 1960
RUSSELL, Douglas 1948–50, 1952
RUSSELL, Marilyn C. 1954
SACKS, Betsy Lee 1966–68
    aka HAMILTON, Betsy Sacks
SALINGER, Diane 1974
SALISBURY, David 1977
SALSBURY, Baker 1965–66
SALTUS, Carol 1952–53, 1955
SALTUS, Janet 1952–53
SALTUS, Richard 1954–56
SALVATORE, Bruce 1963
SAMPELS, Dave 1966
SAMPSEL, Curt 1983
SAMSON, Jack 1947
SANBORN, Jane 1968
SANCHEZ, George 1962
SANDERSON, Jack 1935
SANDOE, Anne L. 1954–55, 1958
SANDOE, James 1948–51, 1954
SANDOE, Jill Ellen 1954–55, 1958
SANDOE, John 1954–55, 1958, 1960–61
SANDOE, Julia 1957
SANTO, Michael 1977–78
SATTERLEE, David 1948
SAUERS, Riley 1964
SAUNDERS, Patricia 1953
SAVAGE, Neil 1972–73, 1975

SAWYER, Elaine 1968, 1970
SCALES, Clydine 1978, 1980–83
SCALES, Thomas Arthur 1977–81
SCHAFFER, Marjorie 1955
SCHANDER, Larry 1952–53
SCHAUB, Randy 1978–79
SCHERER, Douglas 1972
SCHESVENTER, Robert 1957
SCHMIDT, Inge 1954
SCHOTT, Melita 1984
SCHROEDER, Gregory Ward 1970–71
SCHUCHARD, Richard 1939–40, 1950
SCHUERMAN, Sandra 1960
SCHULER, Barbara Jean 1939
SCHULER, Mary 1936
SCHULTZ, Mark 1971
SCHWARTZ, Matt 1982–84
SCOLMAN, Michael 1969
SCOTHORN, Robert A. 1949–50
SEAL, Karen 1972–73
SEDEY, Carolyn 1953
SEELEY, Mark 1939
SEIBER, Suzanne 1971
SEITZ, Lee 1951
SELBY, Jeanne Fabrick 1935
SETRAKIAN, Donna 1962, 1964
SHANAHAN, Don 1940
SHANDRO, Hutchison 1961
SHARP, William 1957
SHEEHAN, John 1970
SHELDON, Jim 1957
SHELDON, Susan 1971
SHELLABARGER, Jill 1980
SHELTON, Timothy 1967
SHEPARD, John 1977–80
SHEPHARD, William 1965
SHEPHERD, John 1968
SHEPHERD, Powell 1963
SHERMAN, Norville 1964
SHEVLIN, Rosemary 1967
SHINE, Stephanie 1984–85
SHIVELY, Sally 1959–61
SHIVELY, Susan Leigh 1949, 1955–56
SHIVELY, Thornton T. 1948–49, 1951
SHOOK, Warner 1974
SHOOKHOFF, David 1965
SICULAR, Robert 1982–84
SIFDOL, Sally Jean 1960
SILBERT, Peter 1973–75
SILVA, Art 1956
SINCLAIR, Wallace D. 1958

SINE, Jack 1966
SINGLETON, Robert 1968–69
SKERRY, Cindy 1965
SKUDLAREK, Marsha 1971
SLEIGHT, Richard 1937
SLETTELAND, Myshkin 1969
SLOAN, Gary 1978–80
SLOANE, Don 1938
SLOVER, Patricia 1980–81
SMART, Jean 1975–77
SMITH, Auriol M.D. 1959
SMITH, Bo 1977–78
   aka SMITH, Robert
SMITH, Brad 1976
SMITH, Candice 1948
SMITH, David 1977
SMITH, Dennis 1968–69, 1981
SMITH, Emmy Lou 1940
SMITH, Frank 1937–38
SMITH, George Francis 1935–38, 1940
SMITH, James 1963
SMITH, Latimer 1964
SMITH, Laurie 1965
SMITH, Marion 1963
SMITH, Mark 1978
SMITH, Noni 1950
SMITH, Richard G. 1950
SMITH, Robert 1977
   aka SMITH, Bo
SMITH, Wayne 1936
SMYTHE, Sally 1979–80
SNEED, Philip Charles 1984–85
SNELL, Norma Jeanne 1950
SNIDER, Robert 1949
SOESBE, Doug 1969
SOLEM, Delmar 1939–40
SONDERSKOV, Diane 1960
SOPYLA, Ronald Stanley 1977
SOULE, Donald E. 1955
SPARKS, Dennis 1966–67
SPARKS, Marion 1951
SPARKS, Melba Day 1938
   aka DAY, Melba
SPARROW, Harriet 1939
SPICKARD, Nelsen Beim 1982
SPINDT, Carla 1985
SPRINGER, Anya 1979
STABLER, Sara 1949
STAHL, Mara Manly 1965–66
STAMBLER, Sarah Elizabeth 1963
STANCLIFFE, Kathryn Denzer 1938, 1940

STARCHER, Robene 1950–52
STARK, Jon Marr 1953
STATLER, Vernon 1967
STATTEL, Bob 1955
STEARNS, Stephen 1968
STEDMAN, Audrey Lofland 1935–39
STEDMAN, Lois 1964
STEDMAN, Robert 1935–39
STEELEY, Brian 1970
STEIN, Daniel 1981
STERLING, Edna J. 1972
STERLING, Jay Theodore 1967
STERNE, Richard 1963
STETSON, Lee 1974
STEVENS, Jane 1960–61
STEVENS, Wilber 1939
STEVENS–JONES, Jane 1976
STEVENSON, Elmo 1947
STEWART, Ernie 1973–74
STONE, Eric 1982–84
STOTHERS, Randall Eugene 1967–68
STRANGE, Fred 1957, 1960
STREITZ, Marilyn 1947
STROTHER, Clista Towne 1978
STROUD, Walter 1980
STUART, Randall 1981–82
STUART-MORRIS, Joan 1979–85
STUCKEY, Jimmy 1951–52
STUCKEY, Johnny 1951–52
STUDACH, Dave 1971–72
SUMEARLL, Eric 1984
SWANSON, Boyd 1939
SWANSON, Jack J. 1954–56
SWEARINGEN, John W. 1958, 1969–70
SWENSON, David 1963
SYLLIAASEN, Terry 1950
SYMONDS, Jan 1954
SYMONDS, Robert 1954
TABER, Charles 1976
TANQUERY, Leland 1968
TARA, William 1964
TARVER, Milt 1965, 1967–68
TATE, Kamella 1984–85
TATE, Karen 1966–68
   aka BOETTCHER, Karen Sue
TATE, William 1968
TAYLOR, Charles G. 1960, 1962–63
TAYLOR, George 1969
TAYLOR, John E. 1950, 1952
TEBBE, Geraldine 1949
TEETERS, Mark 1982

TEMBECK, Robert 1963
TEMPLE, Gregory Scott 1970–71
TERKUILE, Bill 1979–80
THAYER, David 1955
THAYER, Marcia 1957
THOMAS, Dorothy 1938
THOMAS, Eberle 1956
THOMAS, Mary Ellen 1982–83
THOMPSON, Brian 1976–77
THOMPSON, David 1984–85
THOMPSON, Julia 1963
THOMPSON, Lester 1964
THORNTON, Kirk 1979–80
THORNTON, Michael 1954
TILSON, Alan 1972
TIPPIN, Martha J. 1971
TOBIN, William 1947
TODD, Hal J. 1956
TOMARAS, Diamando 1959
TOMPKINS, James Roy, III 1971
TOWERS, Robert 1958–59
TOWNLEY, Julie 1962
TOWNSEND, Gordon 1976–77
TRACY, Emily 1966
TRETSVEN, Marcy 1965
TRIPP, James 1962
TULLOCH, Joe 1969
TURNER, Jerry 1957–60, 1962, 1966, 1972
TURNER, Jo 1957, 1960
TURNER, Mary 1966, 1972–80, 1982–85
   aka YOUNG, Mary
TURNER, William 1975
TYRRELL, Brian 1984–85
TYSON, John Warren 1976–77
UECKER, Harriet 1940
UHERBELAU, Angela 1984
URY, Elizabeth 1985
VAFIADIS, George 1957–59
VAFIADIS, Margaret 1957–59, 1975, 1977–80,
   1982–83, 1985
   aka RUBIN, Margaret
VAIL, Tom 1960, 1963–64
VAN DIJK, Margaret 1975
VAN FOSSEN, Scott 1968
VAN GRIETHUYSEN, Ted 1956
VAN HESSEL, Richard 1979, 1981, 1983
VAN HOOSER, Jolene 1970
   aka PHELPS, Jolene
VANDER SCHAAF, Julia 1981
VANDEVORT, Edgar 1960
VAWTER, Jerry 1940

VEAZEY, Cindy Kay 1967–68
VELTON, Leslie 1975, 1977
VEST, Rudolph E., Jr. 1950, 1954, 1956–58
VICTOR, David 1951
VINCENT, Joe 1972–77, 1981, 1983–85
    aka DE SALVIO, Joseph
VIOLA, Doris 1956–57
VOGT, Peter 1966
VON BIEBERSTEIN, Mary Kay 1965
VON GLAN, Denene 1973
VON STEIN, Gary 1969
VOORHEIS, Kathy Ingle 1949
VOSS, Stephanie 1972
WAGNER, Margaret 1948
WAGONER, Scott 1968–70
WAIDE, Barbara 1951, 1959
    aka HUGGINS, Barbara
WALKER, Channing 1971–72
WALKER, Elizabeth 1953
WALKER, Irene 1947
WALLER, Mary 1981
WALSTON, Victor 1963, 1965–66
WALTER, Alan 1978
WALTER, Sheldon 1937
WALTERS, Leslie 1976
WALTON, Shirley 1937
WANDS, Susan 1983–84
WARD, Albert 1949–50
WARDENBURG, Mark 1975–79
WARING, Stephen 1964
WATTENBERGER, Elizabeth 1951
WEAKLEY, Karl 1968
WEBER, Richard 1953
WEEKES, David 1952
WEINER, Tom 1979–80
WELLER, Aaron 1975
WELLER, Rachel 1958
WEST, Robert E. 1961
WETTERAU, Trubee 1947–48, 1950
    aka BELL, Trubee Wetterau
WEXLER, Paul G. 1949–50
WHEELER, Alfred W. 1950
WHIPP, Joe 1962
WHISENANT, David 1953–54
WHITE, Douglas 1982
WHITE, J. Steven 1969–71
WHITE, LaVelle 1939
WHITE, Peter 1977
WHITED, Fred 1950
WHITESIDE, John 1981
WHITFIELD, Hubert, Jr. 1955

WHITMAN, Charles W. 1959–60
WHITNEY, Valeria 1939
WICKSTROM, Gordon M. 1956
WILKENS, Claudia 1966–67
WILKERSON, Lachlan 1978
WILKERSON, Vayle Specht 1939–40
WILKINSON, Patricia 1948
WILLARD, Ida 1939
WILLARD, Shirley 1939
WILLIAMS, Bruce 1976–77
WILLIAMS, David 1971, 1976
    aka BOOTH, David
WILLIAMS, Eleanor 1952
WILLIAMS, Greg 1967
WILLIAMS, Henry 1952
WILLIAMS, Misha 1965
WILLIAMSON, Laird 1964–66, 1972–74
WILLIAMSON, Loyd 1970
WILSON, Alta 1949
WILSON, Harlalee 1940, 1947–48
WILSON, Hugh 1956
WILSON, Karen Reiss 1965
WILSON, Katharine 1936
WILSON, Talmadge 1950–51
WINDT, Bernard 1954, 1966
WINDT, Peter 1954, 1957
WINER, Morris 1951
WINKLESTEIN, Rebecca 1961
WINN, Cal 1973–76, 1980–82
WINSETT, Jon 1983
WINSLOW, Nancy 1955
WINSTON, Melba 1940
WINTER, Edward 1961
WINTER, Everett 1962, 1974
WINTERS, Michael 1970–73
WINTERS, Time 1979
WINTTERLE, John 1949
WOLD, Sonja 1981–82
WOMACK, Joyce 1953–54
WOODCOCK, Richard 1947
WOODING, George III 1962
WOODRUFF, Graham 1960–61
WOODS, Ronald Edmundson 1976–79
WOODWORTH, John 1961
WOODWORTH, Nancye 1962
WOOLF, J. Harry 1980–81
    aka WOOLF, Jeffrey
WOOLMAN, Claude 1953, 1958
    aka JENKINS, Skip
WORLEY, Kathleen 1976
WORONICZ, Henry 1984

WRIGHT, Cathy 1968
WRIGHT, Gary 1984
WULFF, Roald B. 1967
WYND, Martha 1961–63
WYNNE, Paul 1964, 1971
YADON, Burke 1940
YARNELL, Richard 1970–71
YATES, Verle 1949
YORK, Mark 1969
YOUNG, Beverley 1935–36
YOUNG, Mary 1966, 1972–80, 1982–85
    aka TURNER, Mary
YOUNG, Rex 1983–84
ZALUD-MACKIE, Douglas 1982
ZALUD-MACKIE, Marguerite 1982
ZAPELL, Lenore 1948
ZELLERHOFF, Valerie 1967
ZENTNER, Rena 1984
ZIMMERMAN, Rachel Anne 1965
ZORN, Dennis 1960
ZUCKER, Grover 1978
ZUG, Douglas 1961
ZVANUT, James 1964

Hank Kranzler

137

Left: Teddy Seymour as Crab,
Angus Bowmer as Launce
and Nagle Jackson as Speed.
Two Gentlemen of Verona, 1957.
Right: Shag finds new
possibilities in the role of Crab.
Larry Martin as Launce.
Two Gentlemen of Verona, 1966.

Dwaine Smith

Crab, created by Barbara Affonso, plays himself; Cal Winn, Launce; and Will Huddleston, Speed, in *Two Gentlemen of Verona*, 1974.
Left: Babes La Roo as Crab, J. Wesley Huston as Launce. *Two Gentlemen of Verona*, 1981.

Dave Brookman

Hank Kranzler

BIBLIOGRAPHY

This book is based on personal memories, conversations with innumerable friends, and formal records — minutes, reports, letters, newsclippings, scrap books, photographs, programs, and "Oral History" typescripts — preserved in the Archives of the Festival, organized by Nora Yeoman. In addition, the following published works have been consulted:

Atwood, Kay. *Jackson County Conversations*. Medford, Oregon: Jackson County Intermediate Education District, 1975.

Billings, Homer. *The Story of Chautauqua in Southern Oregon*, 1959. Typescripts in Xerox in Library of Southern Oregon State College, Ashland.

Bowmer, Angus L. *As I remember, Adam: An Autobiography of a Festival*. Ashland: The Oregon Shakespearean Festival Association, 1975.

O'Harra, Marjorie. *Ashland, The First 130 Years*. Jacksonville, Oregon: The Southern Oregon Historical Society, 1981.

Oyler, Verne William, Jr. *The Festival Story: A History of the Oregon Shakespearean Festival*. Ann Arbor, Michigan: University Microfilms, 1971. A Dissertation at the University of California, Los Angeles.

Payne, Ben Iden. *A Life in a Wooden O: Memoirs of the Theatre*. New Haven: Yale University Press, 1977.

Speaight, Robert. *William Poel and the Elizabethan Revival*. London: William Heinemann, 1954.

Tate, Hilary. *A Space for Magic: Stage Settings by Richard L. Hay*. Ashland: The Oregon Shakespearean Festival Association, 1979.